Pawhammer Banjo

Three-Finger Clawhammer for Bluegrass, Melodic Style, and Ragtime

by
Steve Kahn

Cover image: "Banjo Cat", Louis A. De Ribas, photographer. 19th century.
Image kindly provided by Archives and Special Collections, University of Montana at Missoula.

WWW.MELBAY.COM

Preface

If you already play clawhammer banjo, but would like to vastly expand the amount of material that is playable in the style, this book will show a way it can be done. To name but two unexpected new things one can play using "pawhammer banjo":

--Scruggs rolls

--Ragtime and later jazz styles

I hope you get as big a kick from learning this technical extension as I had in developing it!

--Steve Kahn

Note

To spare left-handed players from having to mentally reverse descriptions of hands, I use these conventions to refer to the hands:

--"Playing hand": the right hand for a righty, the left hand for a lefty

--"Fretting hand": the left hand for a righty, the right hand for a lefty

About the Author

Steve Kahn has had a varied life in music, from taking up guitar and bass guitar in high school and playing in rock and jazz groups, to pursuing cello study and playing in chamber music groups such as trios and quartets, to obtaining a composition degree from the San Francisco Conservatory of Music, and thence to beginning a new career as a classical and opera singer in the San Francisco Bay Area (singing roles with such companies as Pocket Opera, Cinnabar Theater, and Verismo Opera; more information is available at stevekmusic.net). He started playing banjo during the last of these phases—in late 2019, to be exact—and soon after starting to explore clawhammer style in mid-2020 developed the "pawhammer" technical extension described in the present book. (More information is available at pawhammerbanjo.com)

Contents

Part I.......Bluegrass and Melodic Style

Tunes

Part II.......Ragtime

Tunes (all by Scott Joplin except where notated)

Part 1: Bluegrass and Melodic Style

One of the well-known characteristics of the clawhammer banjo style is the unfeasibility of rapid notes played on a higher string after a middle (or index) finger downstroke (**M**). Lower strings are easily obtained by drop-thumbing; but motion to a higher string is limited to various "compensation techniques", so named by noted clawhammer player and author Ken Perlman in his encyclopedic *Clawhammer Style Banjo*:

> *The alternate-string pull-off is the first (and probably most efficient) of several techniques that are designed to compensate for a limitation of the clawhammer-picking style. (I call these compensation techniques.) Although it is extremely natural to drop the thumb to a string lower than the M-string, it is extremely awkward and difficult to attempt to drop the thumb to a string higher than the M-string.*

I began playing banjo (in three-finger Scruggs style) in late 2019, and discovered the joys of frailing in July of the following year. I soon noted the limitation spelled out by Perlman; and also found the most direct workaround, the **M**-arpeggio, to be both uncomfortable and unsatisfactory.

Casting about for an alternative to this, in September 2020 I began messing around with using either the ring finger or pinky, plucked, as a way out. Rather soon I became very comfortable with the pinky used in this way; and I also liked the symmetry of having three equally-spaced "clawhammer legs" (somewhat similar to the equally-spaced Scruggs fingers, **T, I, M**): the thumb (**T**), the middle finger's nail (**M**), and the pinky (**Pk**).

This book will describe of how to work the pinky into your clawhammer playing, some exercises, and charts of tunes played using this technique which would present possibly insurmountable difficulties employing the compensation techniques described by Perlman in his excellent book.

In addition to opening up all sorts of Scruggs rolls and melodic playing to the clawhammer player, this addition to frailing also makes ragtime (as well as later jazz) tunes quite practical. After the "basic" pawhammer technique is described, its ragtime "cousin" will be covered in part 2 of the book, along with transcriptions of several well-known Scott Joplin tunes.

(Why did I call it "pawhammer"? I wanted a catchy name that's kind of like "clawhammer"; plus, a paw is larger than a claw, and thumb-middle-pinky is larger than thumb-middle.)

How to do it

I initially imagined the use of the pinky (hereafter **Pk**) to be the opposite number of **T**. In Scruggs style one actively picks the strings. Though **T** is in a position to potentially pick its string, clawhammer technique involves it simply coming to rest on its string as a side effect of the **M** striking the string; and then it very passively slides past its string to make its sound. It is not an active Scruggs-type of "picking" or "plucking" at all.

However, while a useful point of departure, this is not quite how the **Pk** gets used. Unlike **T**, it does not come into contact with any string unless it is going to be used in a passage. And when it does play a string, I would describe the picking as a more active motion than that used by **T**. To repeat, if you are, say, going to play an **M** on the second string followed by a **Pk** on the first string, the **Pk** does not come down to the high side of the first string as a side effect of the M striking the second string (as is the case with the **T**). It remains "in the air", poised to stroke the first string from a roughly 45-degree angle above. It should not catch the string too much as it makes contact and passes by. Yet, it should ring as loud as either **M** or **T**.

As you can see in the pictures, my "clawhammer hand" looks like the usual hand, but the pinky is just a slight bit "free" from the rest of the hand (Photo 1). Its angle increases when it is actually going to be used (Photo 3). Essentially, it is free to operate as it wishes without involving the rest of the hand. This may sound daunting. Since I have played other fingerstyle instruments (bass, and classical guitar particularly) I was accustomed to the use of any of the fingers of the (right) hand to play strings. Now when I am playing parts of tunes that don't involve the need for **Pk**, it's just hanging out, not doing anything. But it's loose, and ready for action when needed.

A change of position of the banjo itself may simplify matters, even though it will feel strange. Lay the banjo in your lap, face up. In bringing it up and towards yourself, don't turn it much more than 30 degrees. So it will still feel pretty flat. Adjust this position so the fretting hand is also comfortable. I'd recommend no higher than a 45 degree angle to the floor. (But this is just me. You may find other positions more comfortable. As long as it works, it doesn't matter.)

Preparation and playing, pawhammer style

Photo 1. Preparing to play M-T

Photo 2. Playing M-T

Photo 3. Preparing to play M-Pk

Photo 4. Playing M-Pk

Exercises

Let's start with the most basic use of **Pk**—in alternation with just **M** (**M-Pk-M-Pk**). **Pk** will always follow **M**, (though will not always be followed by another **M**), so by learning this, you've basically got the whole thing wired! Take time with this and practice it very slowly. In particular, after the **M**, wait until the **Pk** starts to do what you are intending for it to do—that is, play the first string. As I said above, the **Pk** does not come into contact with its string as a by product of the **M**-stroke (like **T** does). Now when it pulls past its string (after **Pk**), the hand **does** do exactly what it does when you pull up on a **T**-stroke in clawhammer: the hand "recoils" back to its ready-to-play position (like it's about to knock on a door).

If your hand feels a little unbalanced, see the note on page 19 in Part 2, as well as the pictures there: it's to be expected at first. When you are using only **M** and **Pk**, and leaving out **T**, the hand—used to the clawhammer "bum-diddy" bounce of **T** always being involved—will tend to feel like its "point of balance" (usually between **T** and **M**) has shifted over to the far side of the hand, between **M** and **Pk**. It will become a more familiar physical *Gestalt* over time.

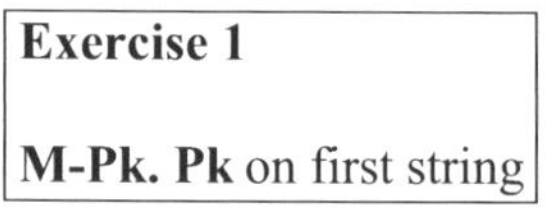

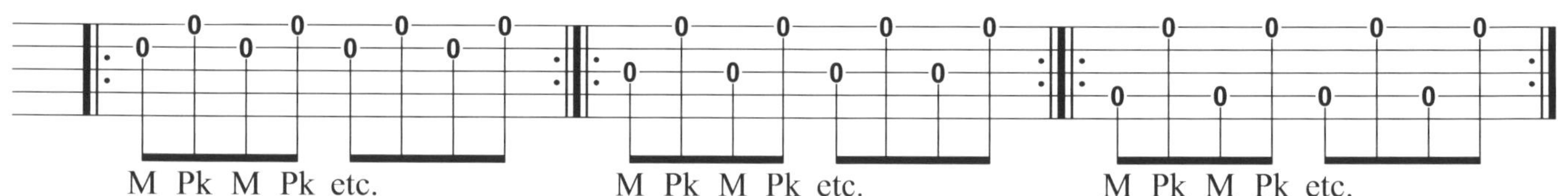

Now that you've got the D string going with **Pk**, let's up the ante by learning it on the second and third strings.

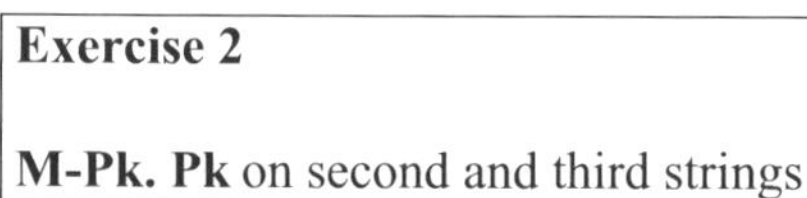

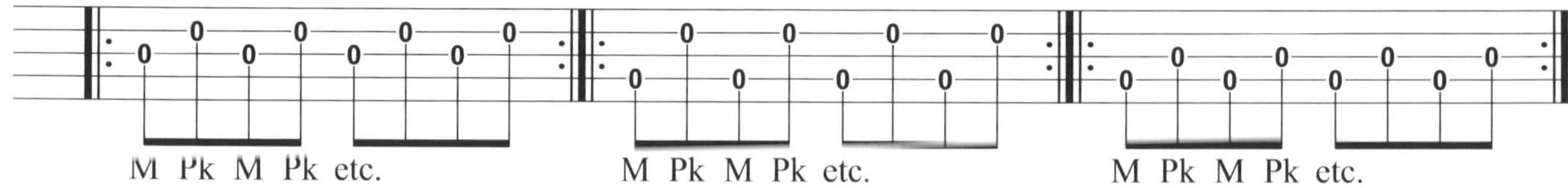

After this, it's pretty much up to your imagination to make up other exercises as needed when playing tunes. One "get comfortable with **Pk**" exercise might consist of playing a "reverse knockdown" style, where instead of playing the melody on the higher strings and inserting a drone **T** on the fifth string on every other note, you play a lower-string melody—on all **M**'s as in knockdown style—and play every other note with **Pk** on the open first string as a drone.

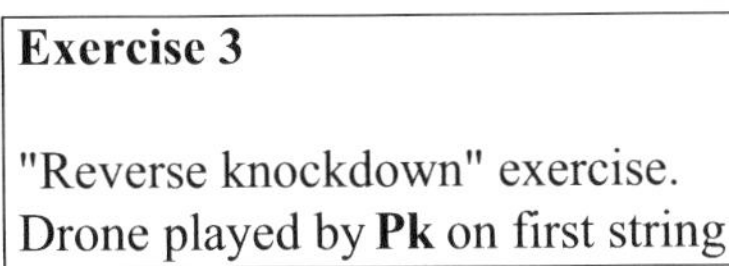

Exercise 3

"Reverse knockdown" exercise.
Drone played by **Pk** on first string

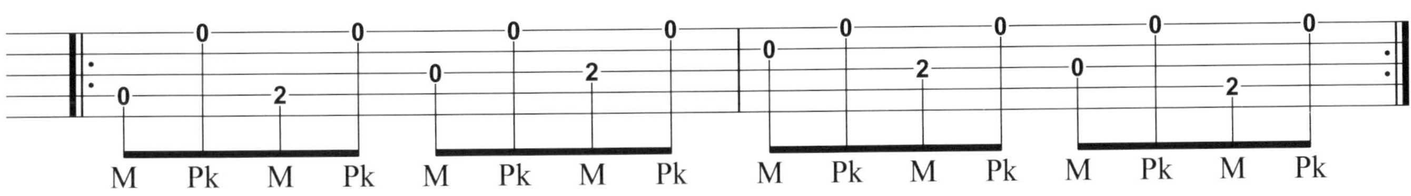

Naturally, hammer-ons, pull-offs, and slides are fully at home with the **Pk**. Here's a short example using all three in this "reverse knockdown" style.

Exercise 4

"Reverse knockdown" exercise with hammer-ons, pull-offs, and slides.
Drone played by **Pk** on first string

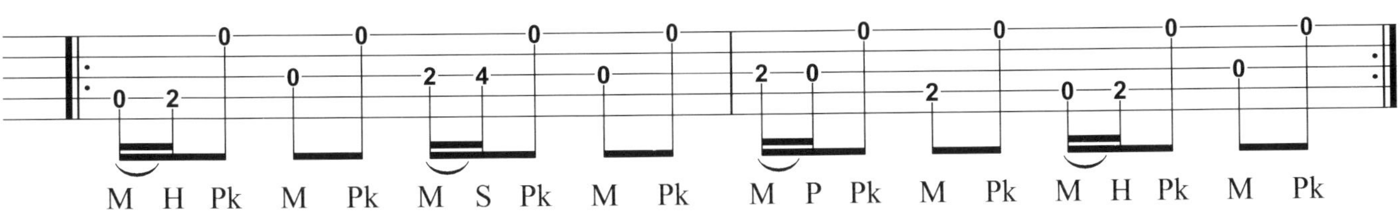

(Note that this "reverse knockdown" style is simply a teaching tool I am using to create illustrations that use the **Pk** in a very regular and predictable way for someone just starting to get the pinky doing what they want it to do. It is not the primary setting for **Pk**, which is to give access to notes otherwise awkward to play in clawhammer style. This will be seen in the song arrangements further on.)

Rolls

One of the big payoffs of incorporating **Pk** into clawhammer style is the sheer amount of "territory" it opens up for the player. Rolls are of course the first thing that comes to mind in this connection; however, there are also patterned runs which, though might not be "roll-like", seem to fall under the same heading.

To become very systematic for a moment, there are (discounting fretting-hand pluckings) three possible "units" of clawhammer play when the **Pk** is added:

1. M-T **2. M-Pk** **3. M-Pk-T**

(Note that a brush, **Br**, may be substituted for **M** in any of these, bringing the total to six; but the more common stroke is likely to be **M**, so I will ignore **Br** here. Anything said below will apply equally well to a roll "unit" with **Br**.)

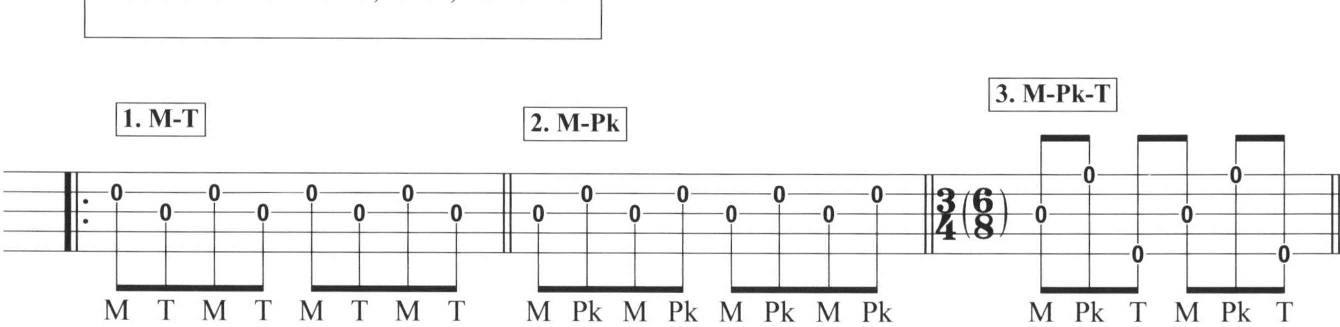

M-Pk-T is as "at home" with songs in 3 as it is in 6/8. Myself, I think of it as a unit of 3 that, in 3/4, just happens to repeat twice in a bar. I don't think of #3 above as **M-Pk,** then **T-M,** then **Pk-T**, because such a sequence makes no sense in clawhammer playing, where **M** is almost invariably the first stroke of any "unit". When practicing **M-Pk-T** try accenting the measure both ways: in 3/4, and in 6/8. The latter will be easier, as the M provides a natural accent. It will be harder to smooth this out in 3/4 so it doesn't sound like "the emph**aaa**sis is on the wrong syll**aaa**ble", as they say. Usually you would simply be picking another set of notes in 3/4 anyway, one that doesn't set up the implied cross-rhythm shown above. But it never hurts to be able to emphasize **T**, or even **Pk**, over **M**...it just might come in handy sometime.

The next step is to consider the roll patterns, which consist of these three basic building blocks strung together in different ways, like railcars in a switching yard. These consist of two types: duple, and triple.

Duple:	**1. M-T…M-Pk**	**2. M-Pk…M-T**
	3. M-T…M-T	**4. M-Pk…M-Pk**
Triple:	**1. M-T…M-Pk…M-T**	**2. M-Pk…M-T…M-Pk**

(Finally, there is the "true triple" pattern **M-Pk-T**, which will be covered in a separate section below.)

It will be seen that the triple patterns do not have anything to do with whether the song is in 3 or not. All the following except one are in 4:

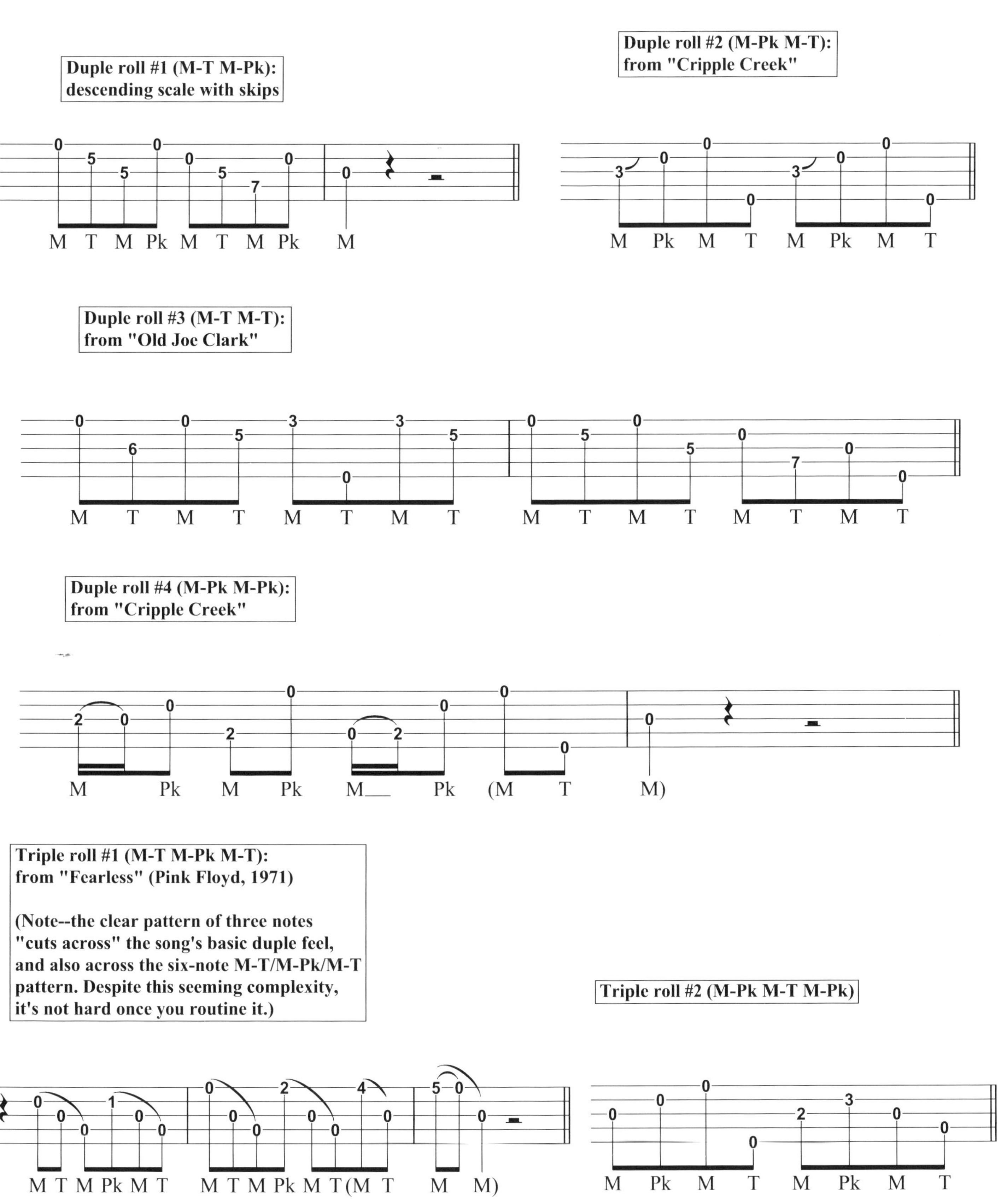

Key to the kingdom: the M-Pk-T pattern

The **M-Pk-T** unit is tricky to play. It requires that you keep **T** in connection with its string after both **M** and **Pk**. The hand does "roll" a bit as **Pk** is sounded, because instead of lifting your hand straight up, as usual, the **T** is still anchored, waiting its turn; and it is all the way over on the other side of the hand. The hand in fact rotates around the axis of the **T**.

This pattern makes playable many standard rolls. Here are a few licks presented side-by-side in Scruggs and pawhammer:

Inside-out roll playable by use of a single M-Pk-T (and subsequent T's on strong beat)

(Scruggs) (pawhammer)

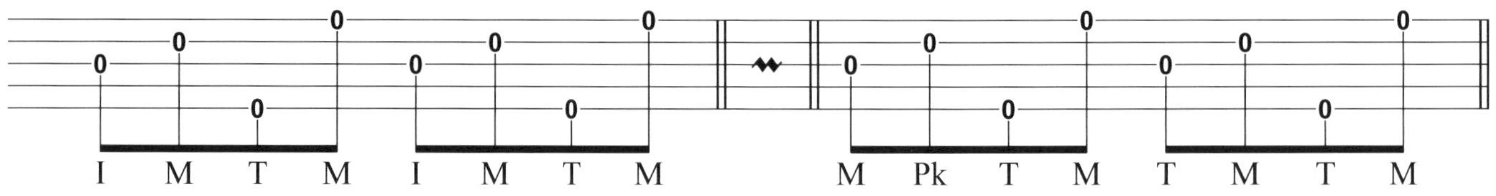

I M T M I M T M
M Pk T M T M T M

Forward roll: M-Pk-T repeated as is I-M-T in Scruggs

(Scruggs) (pawhammer)

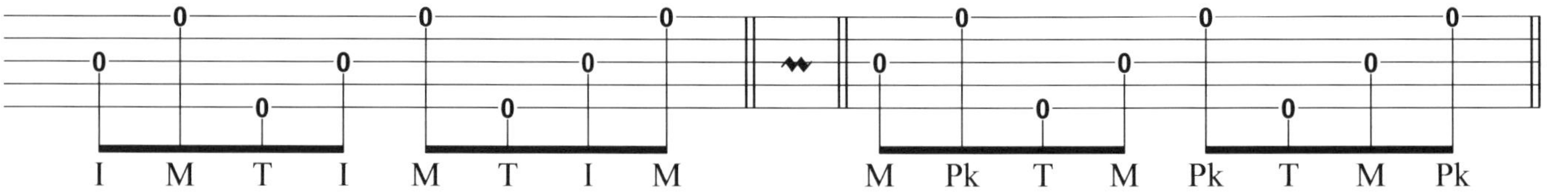

I M T I M T I M
M Pk T M Pk T M Pk

A well-known lick

(Scruggs) (pawhammer)

I M T I - Sl I T P
M M
M Pk T M - Sl M T P*
Pk

(*open 1st string may be played as well with Pk if desired; myself, I leave it out)

The "pinky brush" (PkBr)

In the arrangement of ***Casey Jones*** a few pages on, you will find the notation **PkBr.** More will be said about this stroke in the ragtime section, as it's used a fair amount in ragtime. For now, it's sufficient to say that it's like a mini-*rasgueado* stroke going **upwards.**

Exercise 5

The "pinky brush" **(PkBr)**

Br PkBr Br PkBr Br PkBr Br PkBr Br PkBr Br PkBr Br PkBr Br PkBr

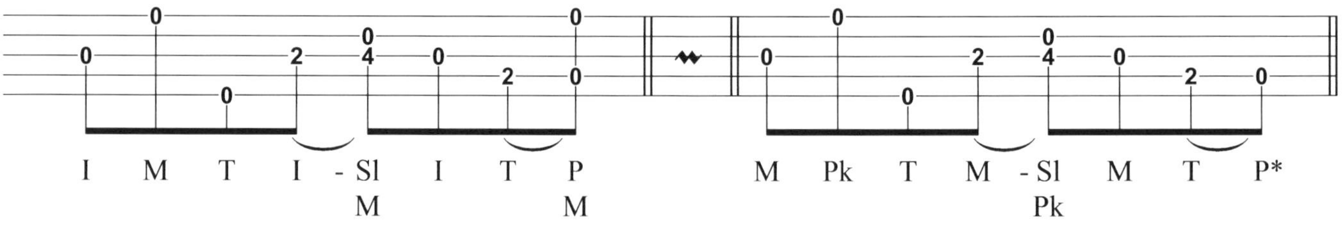

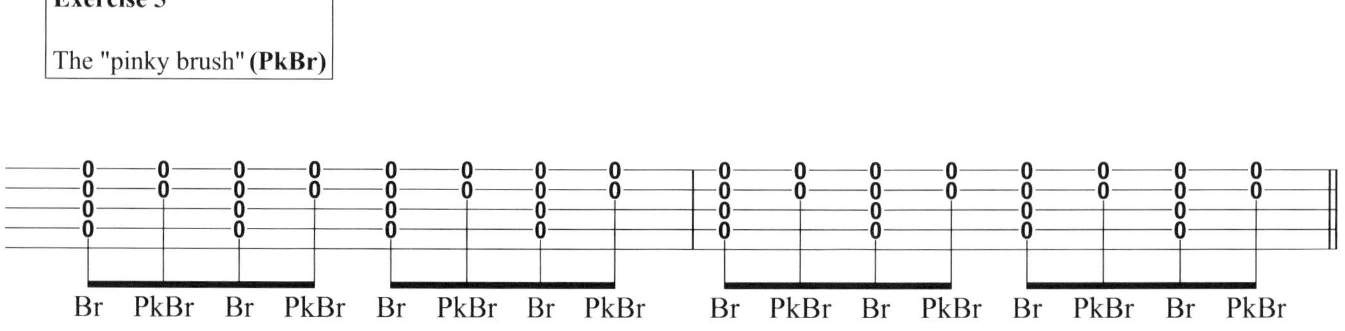

Arkansas Traveler

Traditional
(arr. Steve Kahn)

A

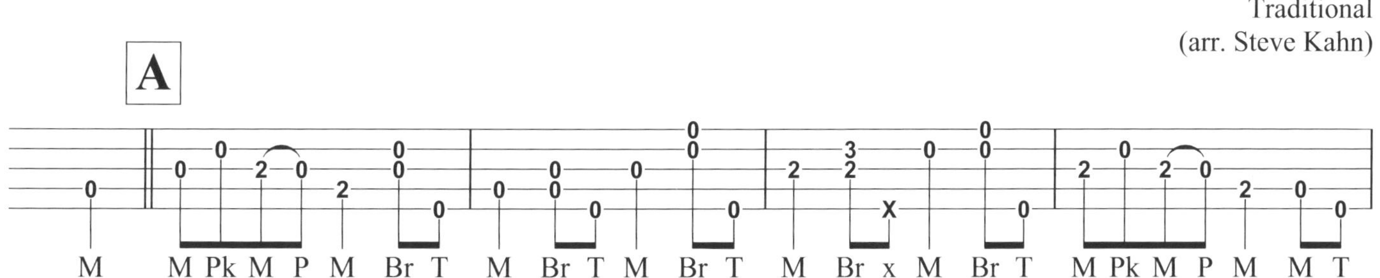

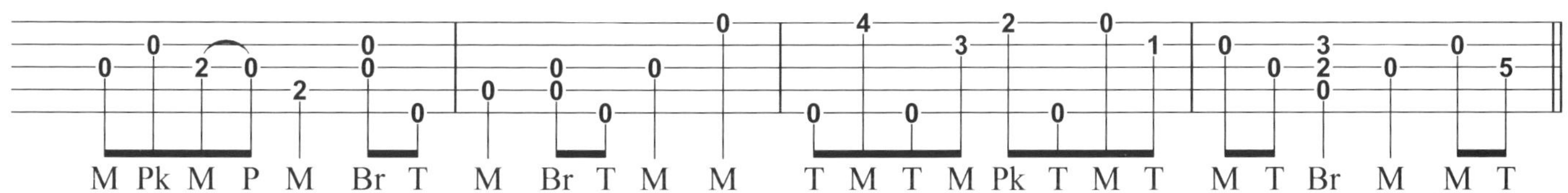

B

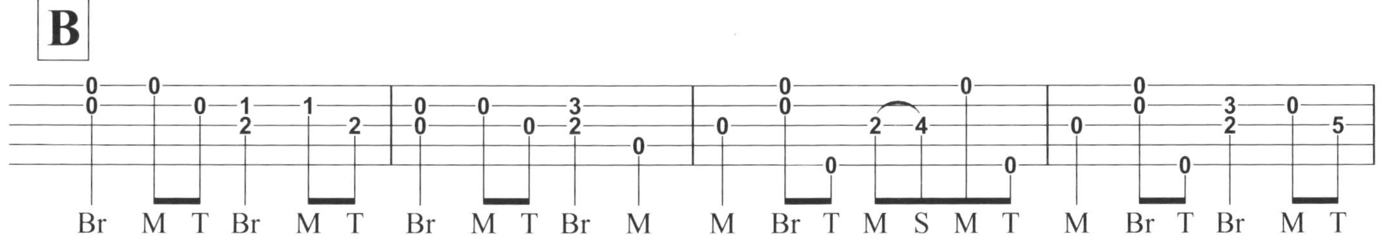

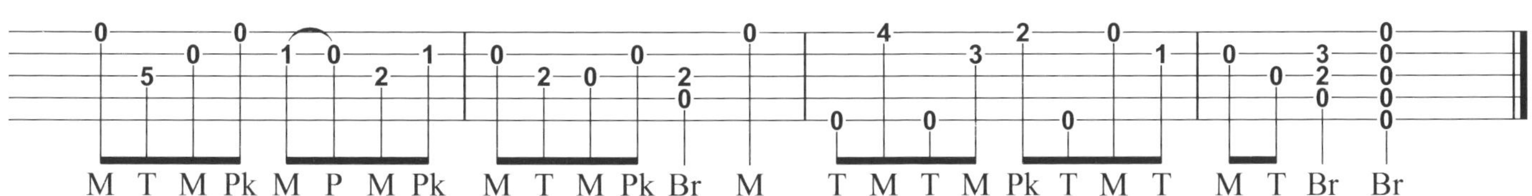

Casey Jones

Traditional
(arr. Steve Kahn)

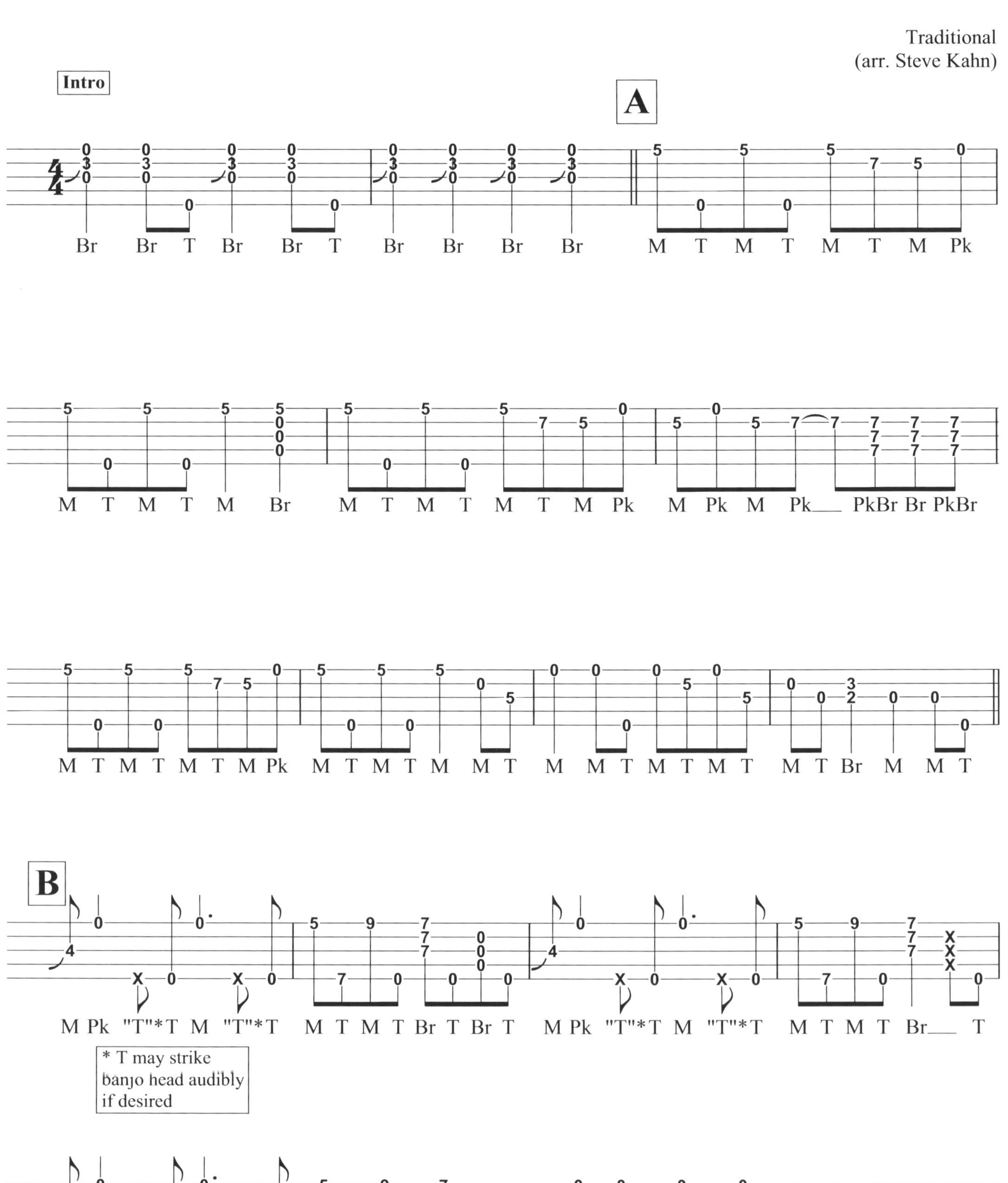

Cripple Creek

Traditional
(arr. Steve Kahn)

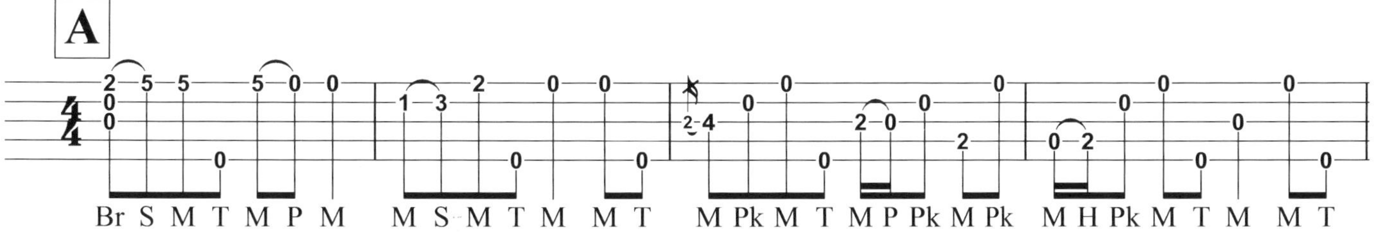

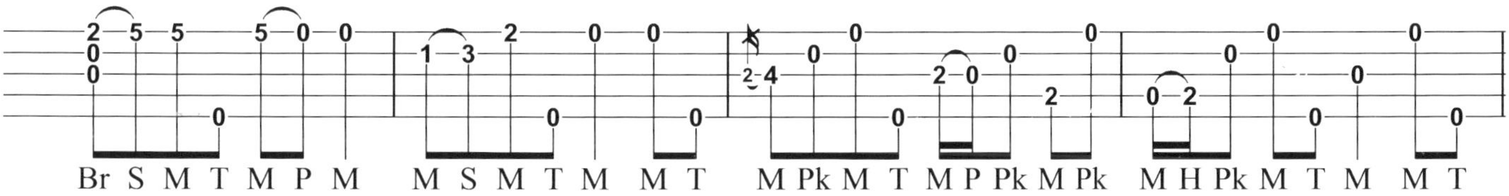

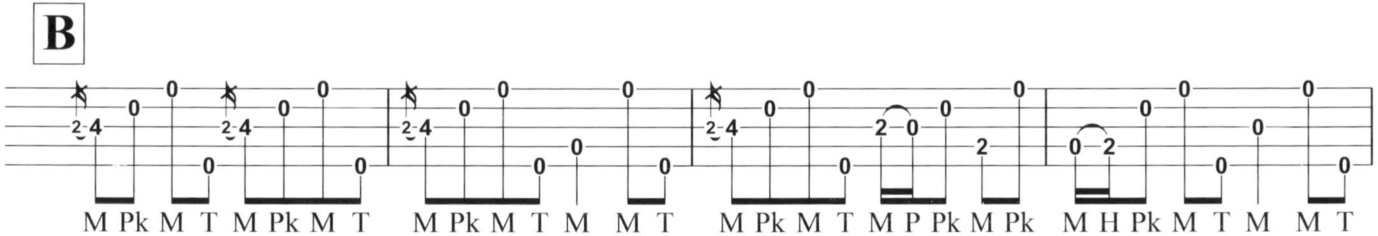

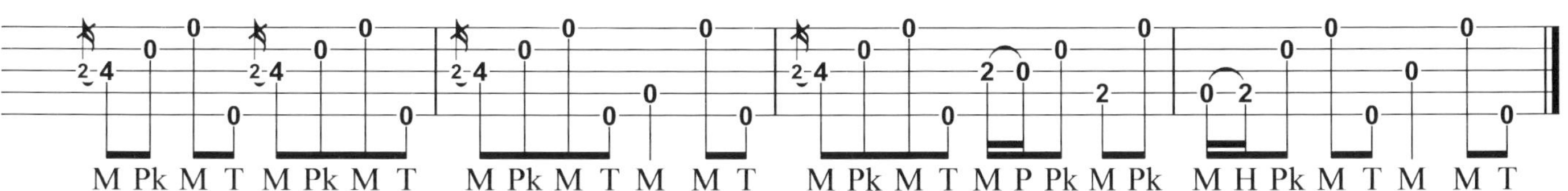

Cumberland Gap

Traditional
(arr. Steve Kahn)

A

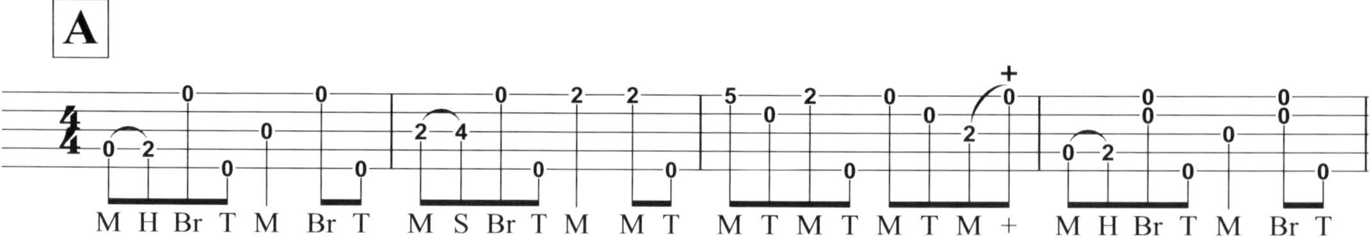

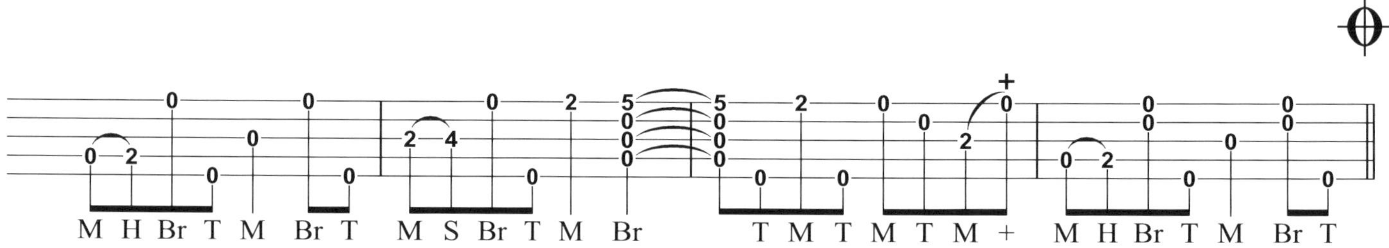

B

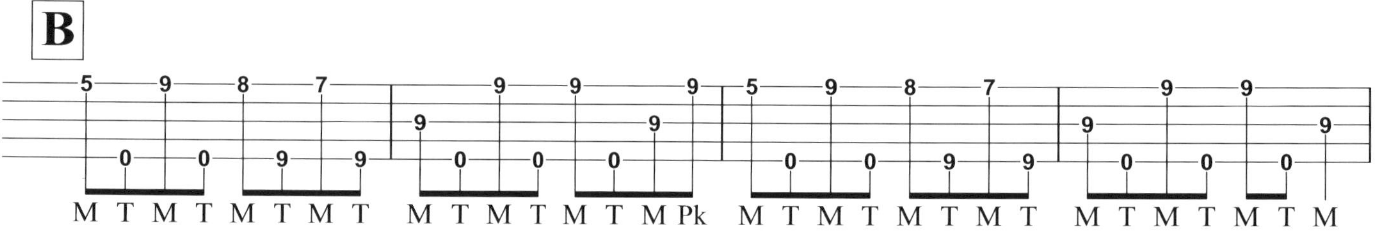

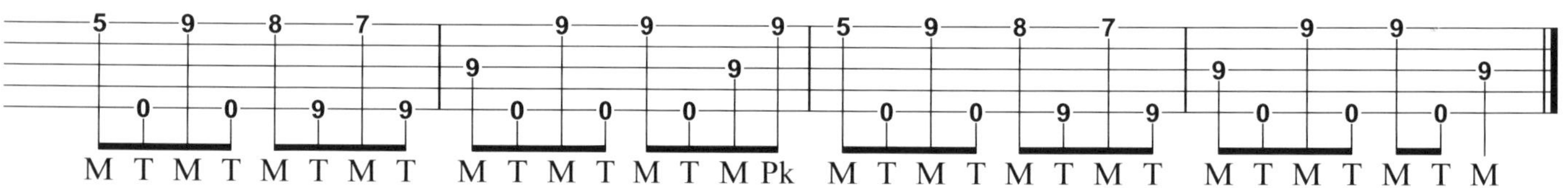

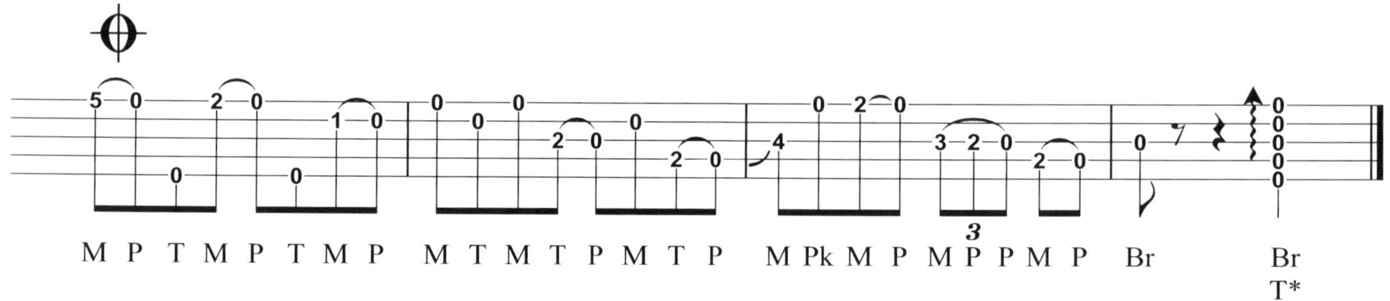

* Play 5th string slightly **after** the open-string brush

Twain Harte Tune

composed and arranged by Steve Kahn

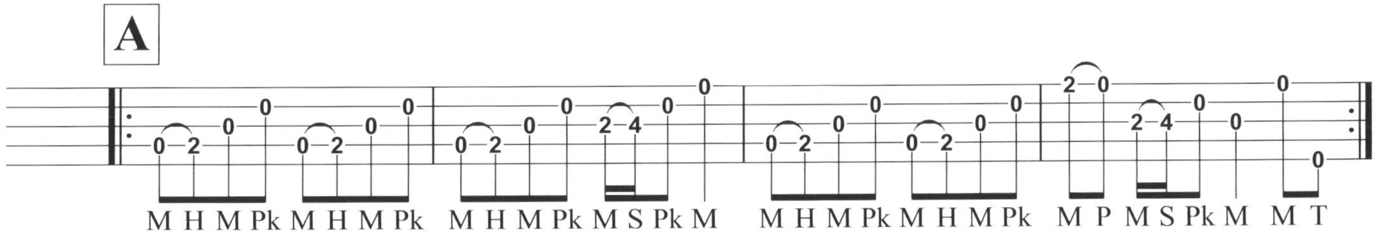

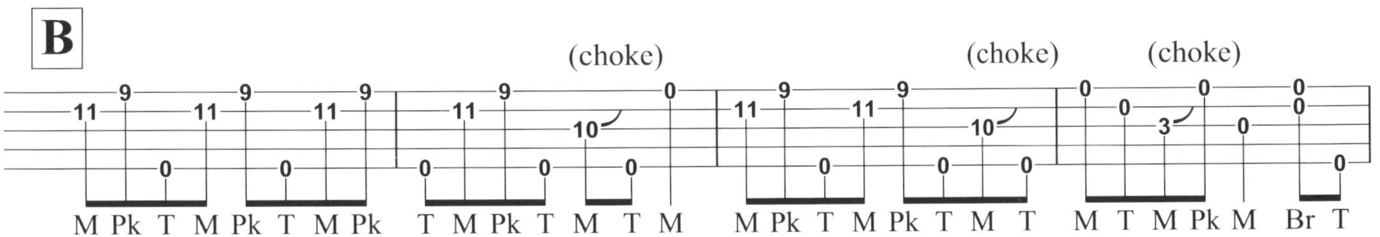

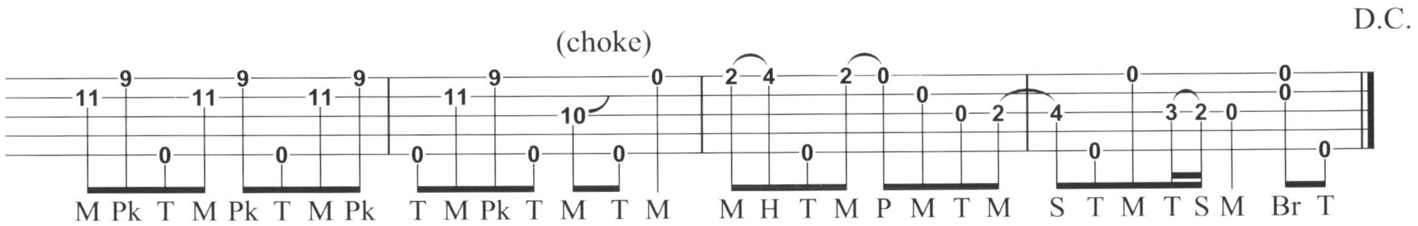

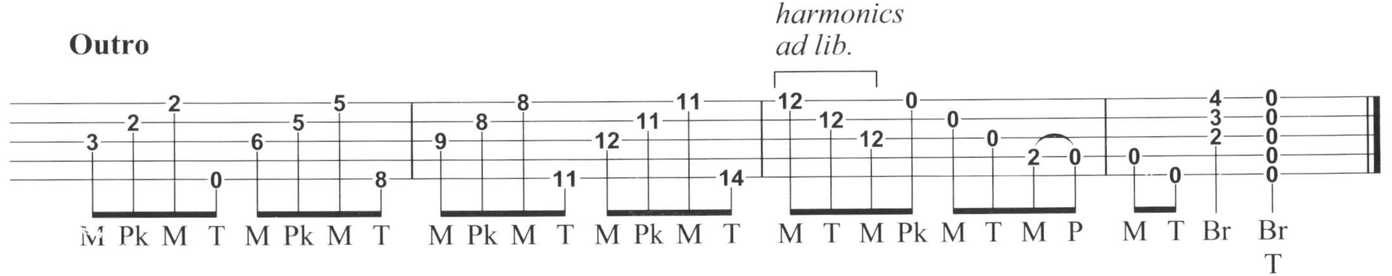

Deputy Dalton

Alan Munde
(arr. Steve Kahn)

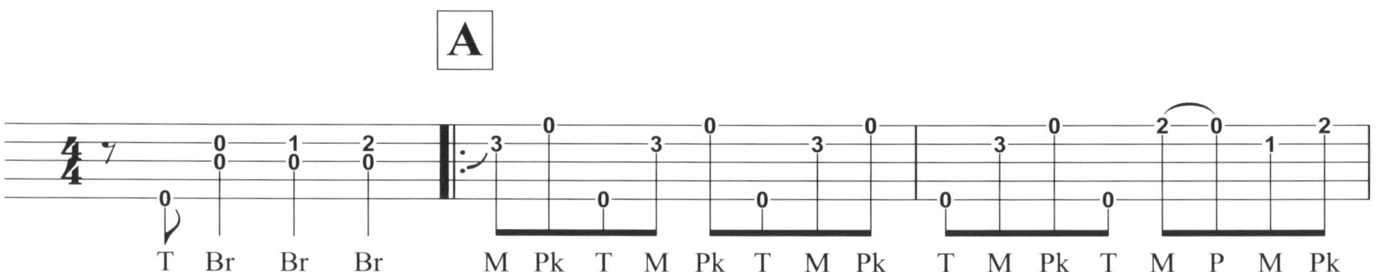

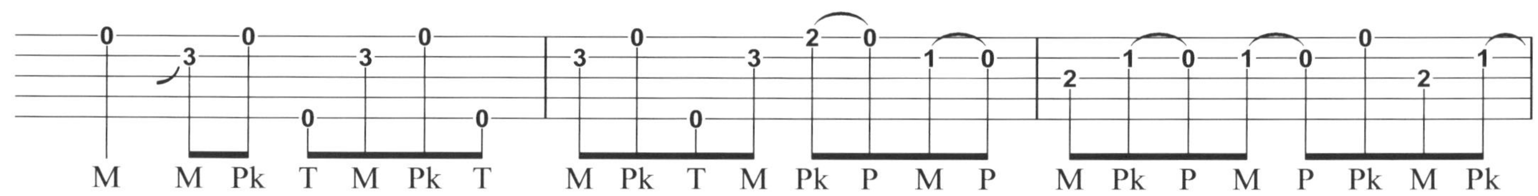

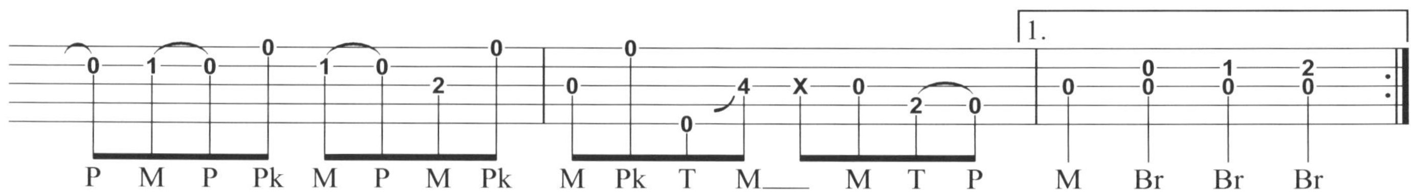

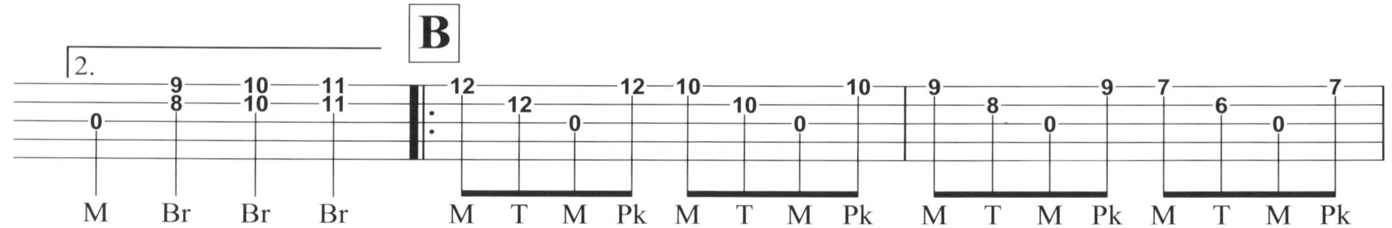

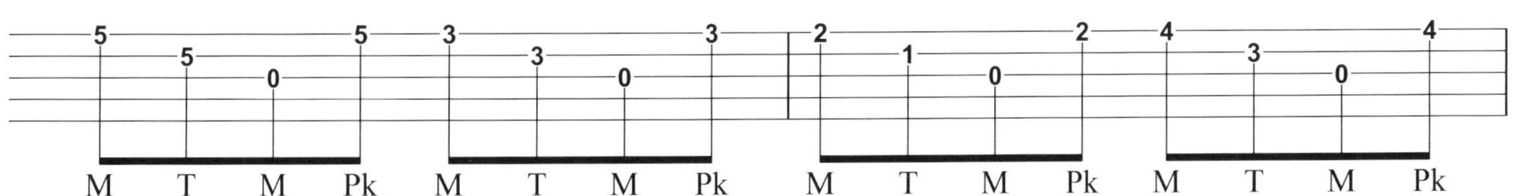

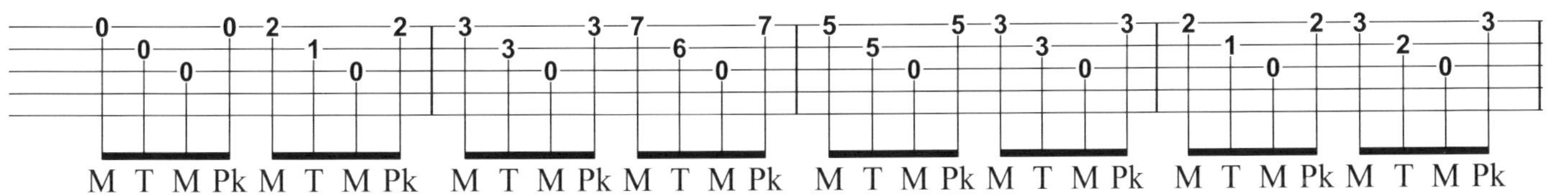

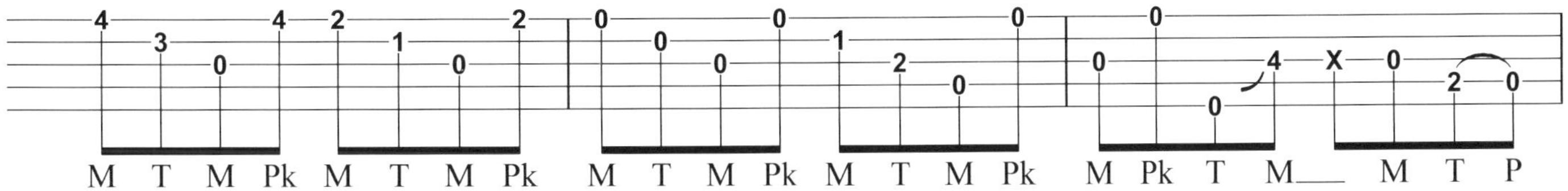

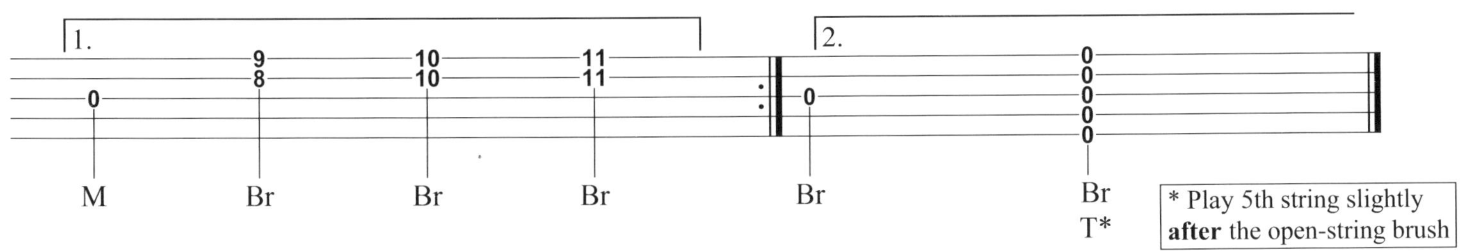
1.
2.
* Play 5th string slightly **after** the open-string brush

Part 2: Ragtime

Ragtime generally does not make use of the "bum-diddy" pattern (**M-Br-T**) of traditional clawhammer playing. Instead, one finds a "chunk-chunk" (or perhaps "oom-pah") pattern—which is printed in the left hand of the original piano part. This "motor" keeps the music going.

How does one achieve this? **Its basis is M-Pk, or Br-Pk.** (You may well recognize this pattern from the "reverse knockdown" pattern I mentioned earlier.)

Example showing similarity of M-Pk to Br-Pk

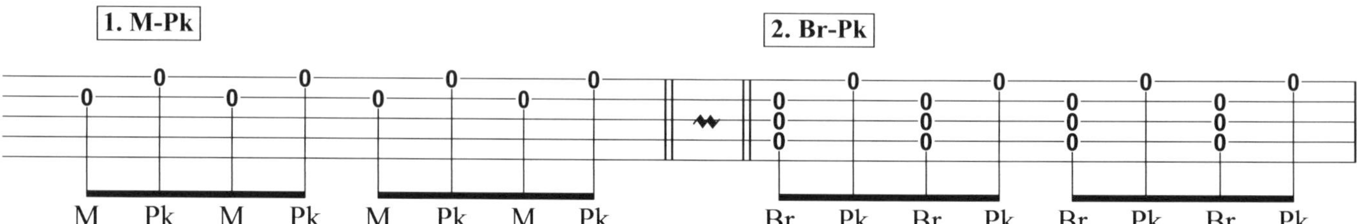

This is a pattern that, while you will find that it does not appear in every measure (or even a majority!) of the arrangements found further on, underlies the heart of every ragtime tune. (Note that this constant eighth-note pulse can be played straight, as Joplin wrote them, or they can be played as swing eighths, as if one were in 12/8 instead of 4/4. Playing them swung is my preference, but this is entirely up to the player. Try them both!)

The **Pk** almost invariably plays on the off-beat; and since ragtime itself is highly syncopated, the notes played by **Pk** are often central to the melody. In no way are they to be "thrown away". You will find that the use of **T** in ragtime tunes is minimal. There are places where it comes in handy, either for the rare "bum-diddy" passage (for example, the C section of the ***Maple Leaf Rag***), or for melodic use (in the A section of ***Maple Leaf***), but **largely it is not used.**

Accompaniment ("comping")

The bedrock aspect of ragtime tunes—and something you are unlikely to have encountered in other styles of banjo playing (other than plectrum banjo) is that there is accompaniment (or "comping") on nearly every strong beat (1, 2, 3, and 4). Below is a simple example, which will be refined in the following pages.

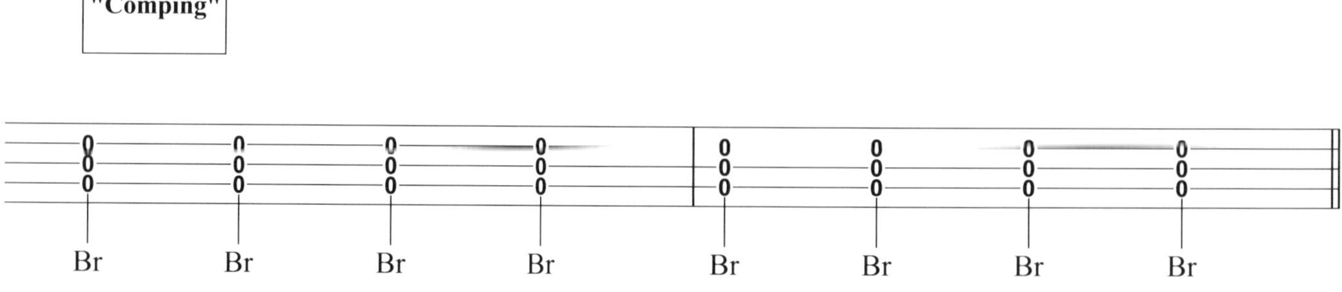

Here is something to keep in mind about comping and its centrality to ragtime (and other jazz styles such as Dixieland, swing, and straight-ahead jazz), hinted at above in my comment about "chunk-chunk" comping found so often in swing of the 1930's: the fact that **M** or **Br** occurs on all downbeats (beats 1, 2, 3, and 4) gives a subtle impression of the Freddie Green four-to-the-bar comping style **even when playing a purely melodic passage!** At the beginning of the B section of ***Maple Leaf Rag,*** the following passage occurs:

Melody giving impression of comping:
from B section of ***Maple Leaf Rag***

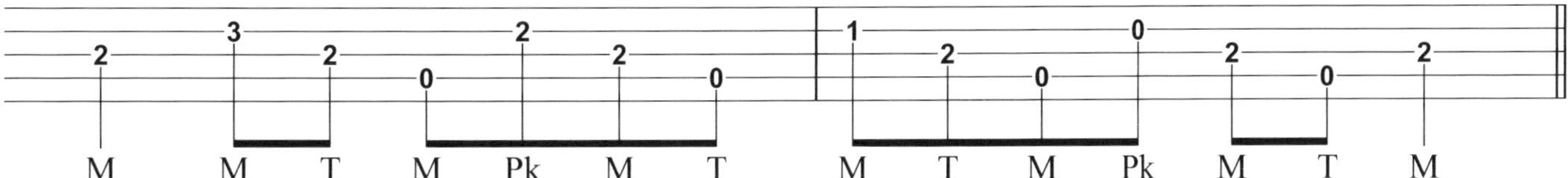

Even though there are no **Br** strokes here, the fact that this passage is preceded (and followed) by comping **gives the illusion that you are still comping.** The constant downbeat **M's** keep the "quasi-plectrum" sound one naturally gets on **M's** and **Br's** (see, for example, the beginning of the A section of ***Pineapple Rag***) during this purely melodic passage. This is merely an observation, however: it is not a suggestion to accent the **M's** here to "bring out" the comping sound. That happens all by itself, as a by-product of the style.

A different playing-hand position for ragtime

There is a small but decisive difference between playing "straight-up" clawhammer with the **Pk** added—so, mostly the familiar "bum-diddy" with the **Pk** coming in for certain melodic notes—and in ragtime playing (or the first exercises in Part I), where use of the **T** is **minimal to non-existent.** (It also occurs in the specific instances where **T** is playing part of a melody ("drop-thumbing")—see the B section of my ***Twain Harte Tune*** in Part I.)

When using the **T** to play the fifth string in a "bum-diddy", the general idea is for the **T** to come down lightly to the side of the string, but not to actually contact the banjo head. You want to be able to keep the bounce going.

But in the instances where **T** is not being used at all, the pinky-side heel of the playing hand pretty much rests on the banjo head, and indeed on the fifth string. (Photo 5) In this style the subtle "balance point" you can feel in your playing hand will be shifted over towards the **M** and **Pk** side of the hand, since those two are doing most of the playing. (In "bum-diddy" playing, on the other hand, this balance point is felt more between **T** and **M,** as those two are doing much of the playing.) I have found that since ragtime playing is both centered on the use of **M** and **Pk** (with almost no **T**), and is played at a slower tempo, the playing hand works a bit better if you feel it turning away from you (along the axis of your forearm) so it feels as if the fingers are more horizontal to the strings than vertical. The **Pk** is played very close to sideways, and with the fleshy tip of the pinky. I found this led to greater accuracy with **Pk**. (Photo 5) (In passages where the **T** does come into play on strings other than the fifth (say, in ***Maple Leaf*** sections A and B, or the turnaround in ***Ragtime Fragment***), if you let the hand turn outwards (away from you) from the wrist ever so slightly, this brings the **T** into closer alignment with **M** and **Pk**.)

This altered balance point makes it natural to have the pinky-side heel of the palm come to rest on the head—it stabilizes the hand, and makes it feel more at home (See the pictures on the next page.). It **also** allows the fleshy part of the side of the palm to **mute** the fifth string, which it will do quite a bit in ragtime (see the next section).

Playing-hand position in ragtime

Photo 5. Ragtime style (T absent):
Heel of hand rests on head; Pk coming in almost sideways

Muting: playing hand

Since **T** is not a big part of ragtime style, the heel of the palm, where that little bone on the pinky side near the wrist is, can nearly **live** on the banjo head right by the fifth string while playing in this style, as stated above. This puts it in a great position to mute the fifth string (and occasionally the fourth string as well). (Photo 5)

When playing passages in G, the muting is not strictly needed; **but** I find that except on the rare occasions in ragtime when **T** is going to play the fifth string, I feel the fifth string against the side of my palm all the time. So I am muting it. Further, ragtime tunes often modulate to the key area of IV and V (C and D in tunes in G), and here, the fifth string **must** be stopped. In fact, there are several tunes which begin in C (***The Entertainer***, for example) and wind up modulating to F. Here, it is absolutely necessary to stop the fifth string from ringing on the Bb chords which occur in passages in F. There are also occasional chromatic passages in ragtime, and here too the fifth string must not sound. Here is such a passage from the second strain of ***Maple Leaf Rag***. (One could do worse than using this passage as a study in stopping the fifth string while playing **Br** on the lower [third and fourth] strings. "If you can do it there", to paraphrase ***New York, New York***, "you can do it anywhere".)

Muting with the playing hand:
from B section of ***Maple Leaf Rag***

etc.

4/5 4/5 3/4 2/3 | 1/2 / / /

Br Br Br Br

(stop 5th string with heel of playing hand)

The damped Br stroke

Another new aspect in ragtime playing is the **damped Br** on the strong beats. If you have played rhythm guitar (especially in funk styles) you will already be familiar with playing a stroke with the pick hand while muting all strings with the fretting hand. It keeps the "chunk-chunk" of the accompaniment going without pitches sounding--a purely rhythmic effect. With the 'clawhammer' hand damping the strings as described in the previous paragraph, this can be done on open strings with your **playing hand** as well as the **fretting hand**. Let the **"Br hand"** simply fall on the strings vertically—and leave out the **Br!** Here is a study of the technique. Do not have your fretting hand anywhere near the fingerboard for this exercise. You will probably get a slight sound out of the third-string G. It should be nowhere near as loud as the open fifth string you are playing on the off-beats, and hence is not objectionable. The quotes around **Br** in this exercise indicate that you're simply dropping the fleshy pinky side of the playing hand onto the strings, with **T** in position for normal clawhammer play:

"Rhythmic" **Br** placeholder
combined with **T**

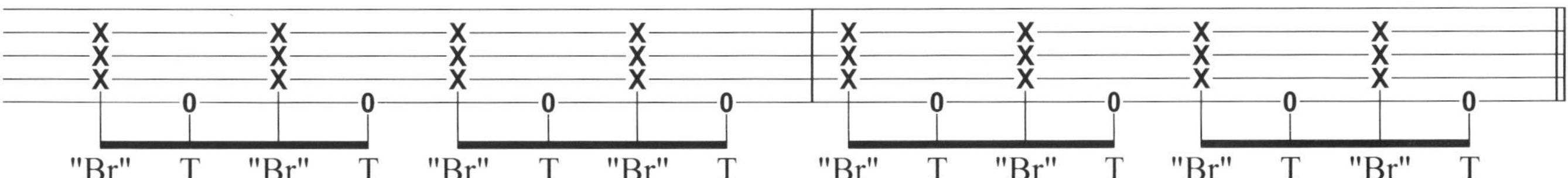

Muting: fretting hand

Another useful muting one can do when playing purely melodic passages is to lightly hook the thumb of the **fretting** hand around the neck and mute the **fourth string (D)** with it. Hook the edge of the thumb lightly around the second fret (or between the first and second fret, or whatever position keeps the fourth string from sounding any pitch at all—see Photo 6, Page 22). (In the picture the thumb is not quite touching the fourth string for clarity in the photography. Of course in actual playing you'll have the thumb actually contact the fourth string, thus muting it.) This should be combined with muting with the playing hand; it's best not to rely on it alone, because the slightest bit of downward pressure with the fretting thumb will give you a note on the fourth string—possibly one you want even less than the open D! Here's an example from the A section of *Gladiolus Rag.*

Fretting hand muting
in A section of ***Gladiolus Rag***

(hook fretting hand thumb around neck so it
lightly stops fourth string (except when playing fourth string)

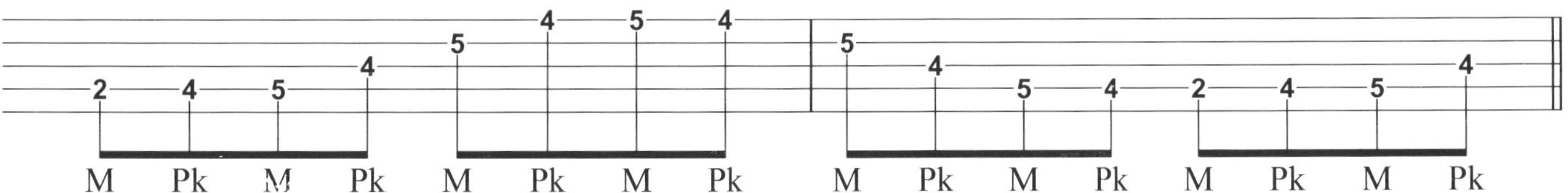

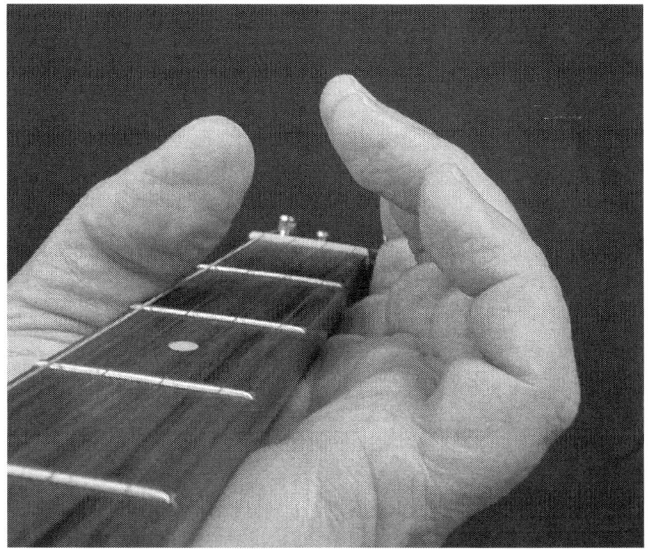

Photo 6. Muting the fourth string with the thumb of the fretting hand

More about the "pinky brush" (PkBr)

The "pinky brush" was first described in Part I. This is a "drag" upward (a mini-*rasgueado*) across the strings on the off-beat. Note that this is of necessity a stroke that "comes off" the strings at a more upward angle. Aim to pull the pinky across in this fashion while the rest of the hand remains bouncing up and down, with the heel of the hand never leaving its "home spot" near the fifth string. Here is a study in the technique. Again, the fretting hand is not to be used. Drop the heel of the playing hand onto the strings as in the exercise in the section above on the **damped Br stroke.**

PkBr combined with damped **Br** stroke

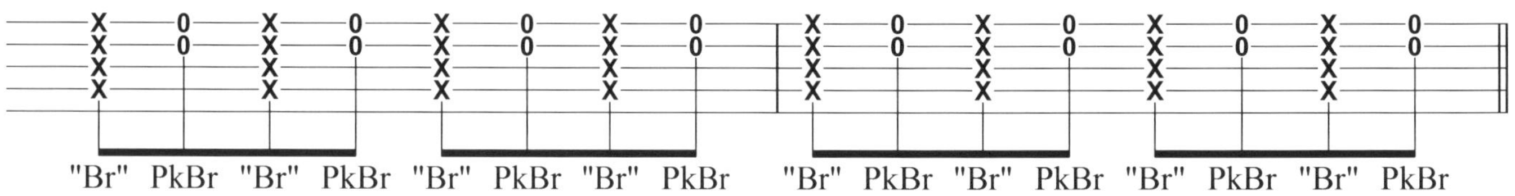

Here's an example (from the A section of ***Maple Leaf Rag***) showing the pinky brush and the damped brush together. (The down arrows indicate the technique's similarity to *rasgueado* in guitar playing.)

Example of damped **Br** stroke in A section of ***Maple Leaf Rag***

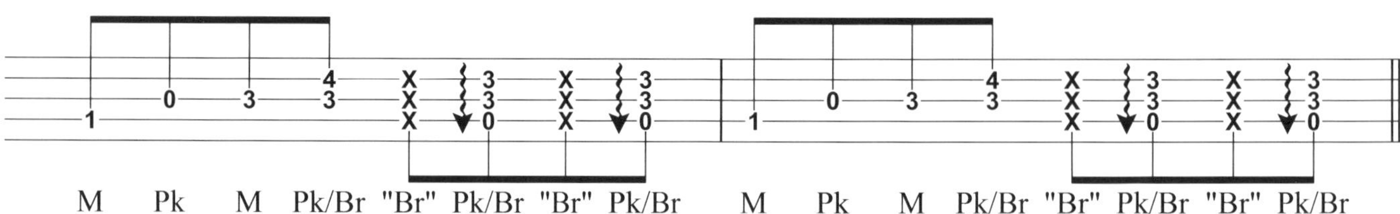

Those familiar with rhythm guitar playing will notice the extra drive these syncopations lend to an arrangement.

By now these examples should make it clear what was stated at the outset of this section: that the soul of ragtime play is the **M-Pk** (or **Br-Pk**) "motor". The **damped Br** on the on-beats is, in a way, a "placeholder" which allows the pulse to continue rhythmically without sounding any notes.

Two-stave notation: why two staves?

Unusually for banjo notation, the use of two staves (instead of one) can be very useful in presenting (and learning) ragtime tunes. The top stave shows the melody, and the bottom one the accompaniment. This is similar to how the original piano part would be notated. In this book the ragtime tunes at the back will be notated in two-stave notation. Here is a passage from ***Maple Leaf Rag*** in both flavors of presentation:

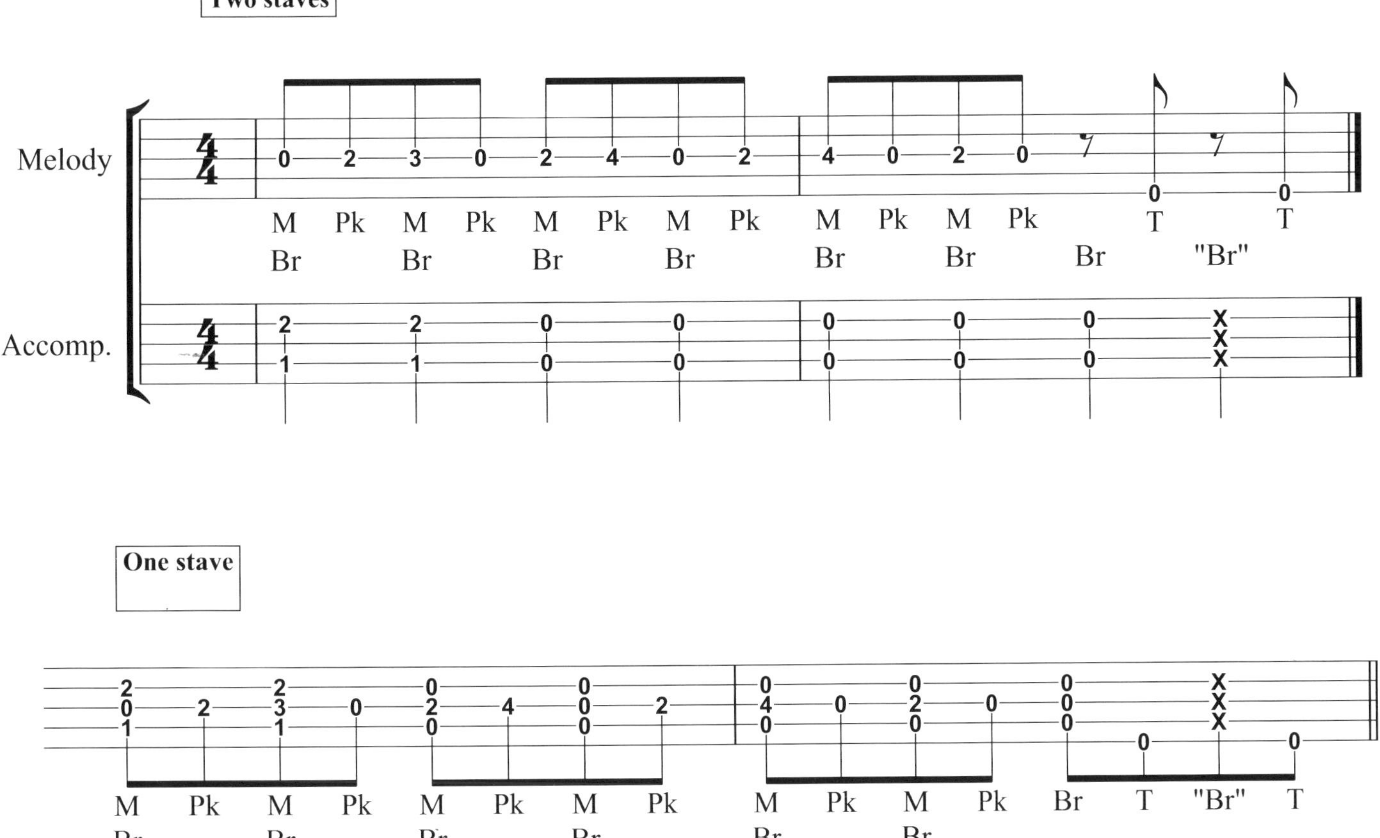

In my view, because ragtime accompaniment can be somewhat "thicker" than in bluegrass, two-stave notation has the virtue of isolating the melody (in the top stave).

By the way: if, while learning a tricky passage, you have to choose between dropping out a bit of melody versus dropping out a bit of accompaniment in a passage while learning it, drop out the accompaniment! The melody is always the boss. An example learned through hard experience while I was learning the A section of ***The Entertainer***:

Melody vs. moving line in accompaniment:
From A section, ***The Entertainer***

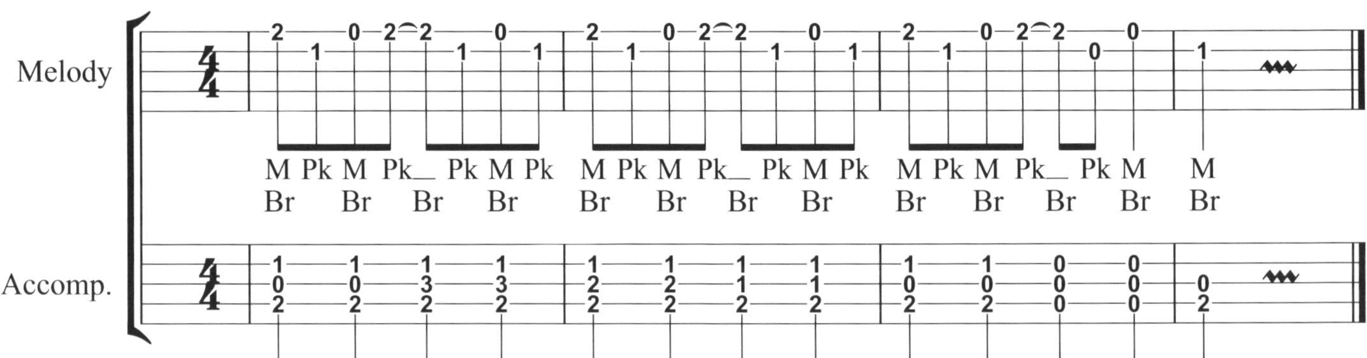

When I first started working on this passage, I overemphasized the "hard part"—the moving line on the third string in the accompaniment. This caused the melody on the top two strings to drop out at times, as I would accidentally mute these strings with the fretting hand in my zeal to get the moving line clear. But when I started ignoring the moving line (partially by a slight rotation of the fretting hand towards the fifth-string side of the instrument in order to make sure the first and second strings didn't accidentally get muted), the passage "worked itself out" and both lines emerged as if by magic!

Something to note from this passage is the near-constant C on the second string, first fret. This pitch serves as **both** an accompaniment note and a melody note here. But there is no contradiction. As a melody note here it is always played by **Pk** on an off-beat (which is, in ragtime play, to say the same thing: the **Pk** plays the off beats); as a "comping note" it is always on a **Br** on the downbeat **while the Br continues on and plays the melody note on the first string in the same motion**.

Here is a study illustrating this on all open strings. The combined **Br** & **M** brushes past the "comping" notes (second, third, & fourth strings) on the on-beat and reaches its melodic destination on the first string **in the same gesture**. A small "flourish" with the fingernail as it goes by the first string and off the strings entirely heightens the melodic effect of the top string. On the off-beats, the third string continues to sound, and depending on whether you are damping the fourth string with the heel of the playing hand, the fourth string may also sound as well.

The curved line on the on-beats is intended to be a visual reminder that fundamentally this '**Br+M**' is one motion. It does not indicate the stroke is to be dragged like a rasgueado, which is instead marked with a squiggly arrow pointing up—see page 29 for an example of that. This *rasgueado* is a nice special effect, which can be used on on-beats like this but is not a basic part of the style. (Note: "*simile*" simply indicates that the marking continues.)

Bringing out the melody while brushing:
Melody on first string of **Br**

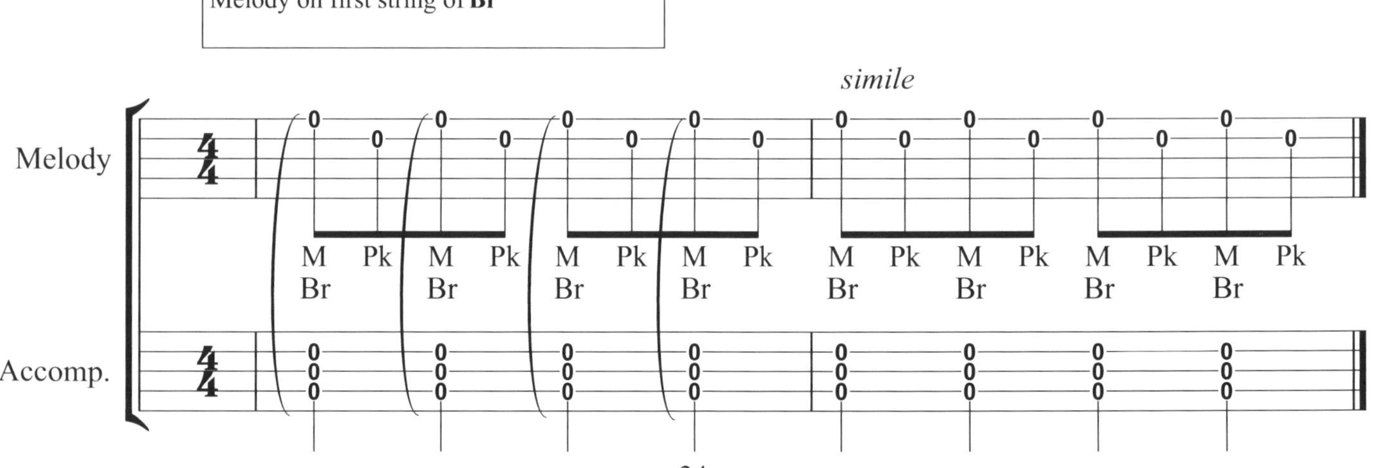

What about when the on-beat melody note is on a lower string than the off-beat? Not a problem. You brush, but "aim at" the melody note. You get two for one! The melody in the following study should stand out clearly against the "chunk-chunk" of the comping.

Bringing out the melody while brushing:
Melody on second string of **Br**

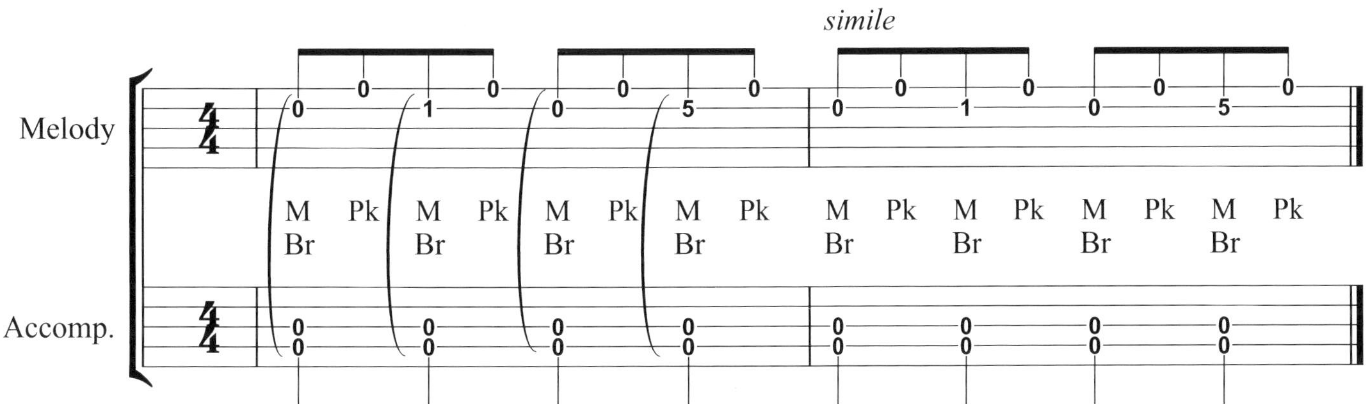

You will notice in the arrangements that at times the notation of the lower stave seems to contain notes that do not match with the notes of the melody. This is due to the fact that at such times, you are holding down a chord form and playing additional notes "on top of" it. (See the introduction of ***Pineapple Rag***, for example.) The accompaniment (lower) stave is close to—but not identical to—if I were to simply notate the melody with small chord form grids above the staff, as bluegrass and folk books do quite often (and certainly plectrum banjo books). However, there is more to this part than meets the eye, and so that is why I have devoted an entire stave to it. The accompaniment stave can be thought of as, "Hold down this chord form, and the melody will weave around it." (Again, for those who have played guitar in rock and jazz bands, this 'melody-weaving-around-a-chord' will be a familiar concept.)

Also, there will be times that the accompaniment is more of a rhythmic stroke with no pitch content. When this happens, the tab notation **of the accompaniment part (lower stave)** is marked with **X**'s. (However, when a ***single*** **X** appears in this part next to numbered notes, it means to stop the brush before it reaches this string.)

Ragtime "bum-diddy"

Well, not really. But there is a general "shape"—I won't go so far as to call it a "pattern"—which occurs in some measures of the tunes below, which gets the comping-on-strong-beats connected with string crossings to create a tapestry not unlike that heard in fingerpicked or flatpicked guitar. Here are several one-measure examples one can round and turn into exercises. But I also include something that points to other musical destinations one can head for with pawhammer: the second example here is basically a blues rhythm guitar riff. (It is interesting to note that the measure right before the first repeat in the B section of ***Solace*** is a similar "shape". If you try rounding just that measure you will see what I mean.)

"Inner riffs":
the first one has a folk/bluegrass feel;
the second is a blues riff.
Note that the **M's** and **Pk's** are the melodic part of each riff.

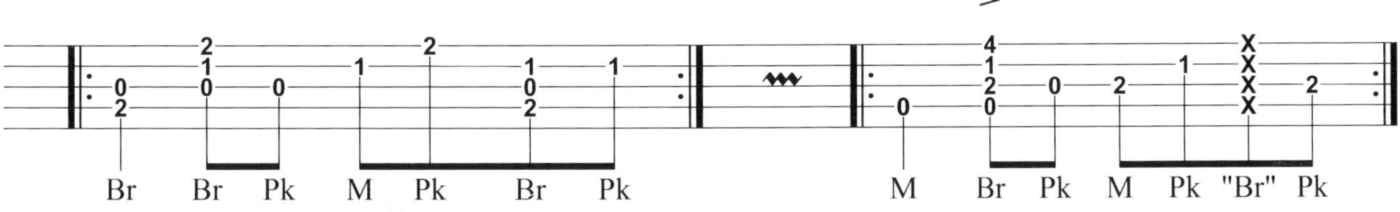

One **can** play an actual "bum-diddy" rhythm using the pattern **M-Br-Pk** (or **M-Br-PkBr)** on strings 1 to 4. Here, the **Pk** is playing the first string just as the **T** would be in regular "bum-diddy" (on the fifth string). This is

extremely useful if playing chordal back-up in tunes that wander away from the chords G and C. In the tunes below, an example of a "bum-diddy" (without **T**) appears in bars 46 and 47—as well as later on in the D section—of ***Maple Leaf Rag.***

Another note

The difference between mostly open strings (sometimes referred to as "arpa") and closed positions (without open strings) is an artistic resource. When you get to a passage with a lot of open strings, you can really go to town and let the instrument ring. An example is the C section of ***Maple Leaf Rag,*** where a little clawhammer "bum-diddy" suddenly breaks out! Without playing with any more force, you get a big shot of energy in the tune for free.

More tunes

Any number of other rags, plus Dixieland, swing, and jazz tunes—basically anything that works with a quarter-note "chunk-chunk" accompaniment, whether the melody is played in swung or straight eighths—work nicely played "pawhammer style". The sky's the limit!

Learning the tunes

It may be best to pick through the **melody** of the following tunes first. Given the chordal simplicity of the accompaniment—and the familiarity of the ragtime style—you will probably be able to hear the accompaniment in your head as you get the melody down. Later, try just playing the accompaniment. By this point you'll probably be ready to put them together.

Scott Joplin
1868 - 1917

The Easy Winners

Scott Joplin
(arr. Steve Kahn)

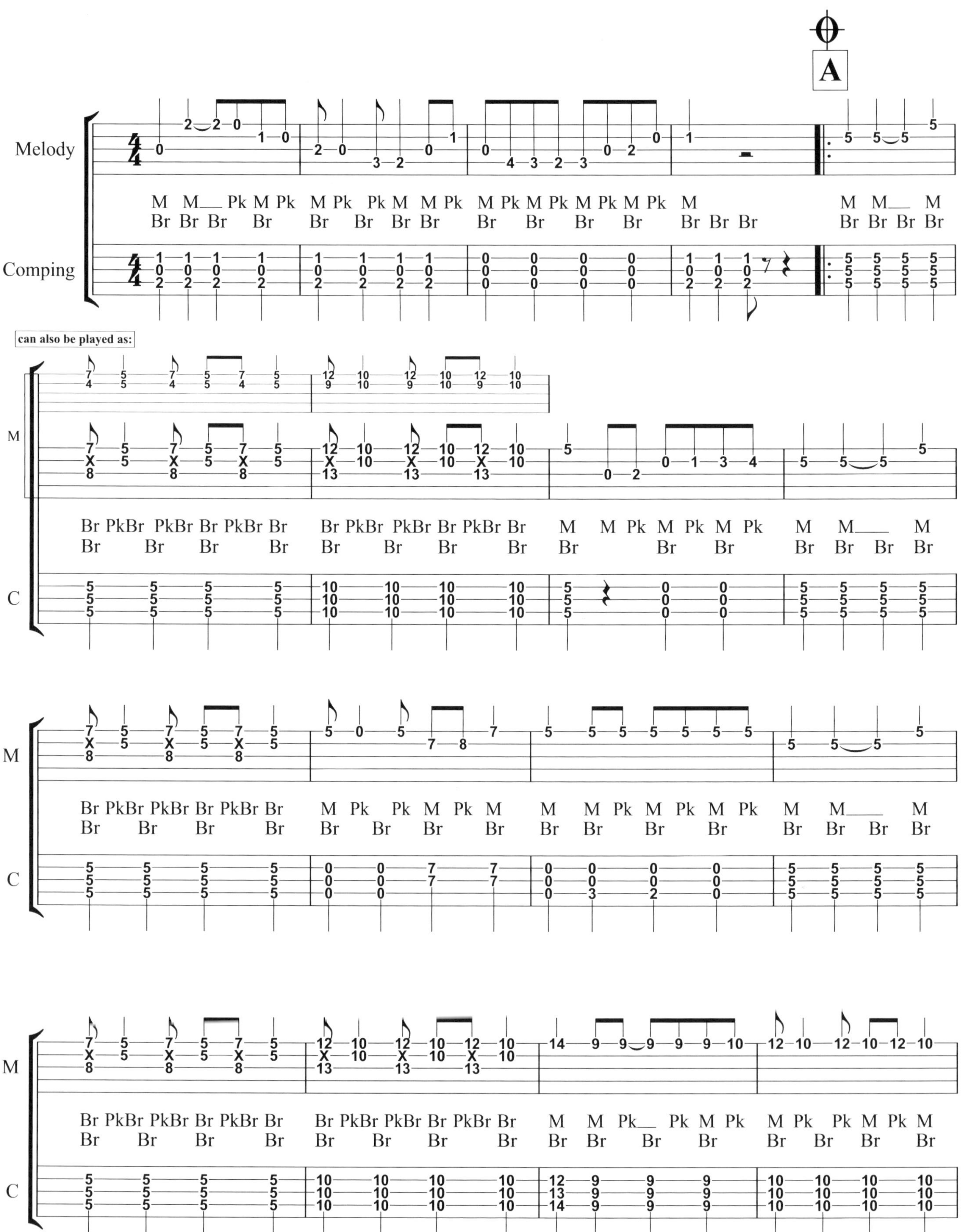

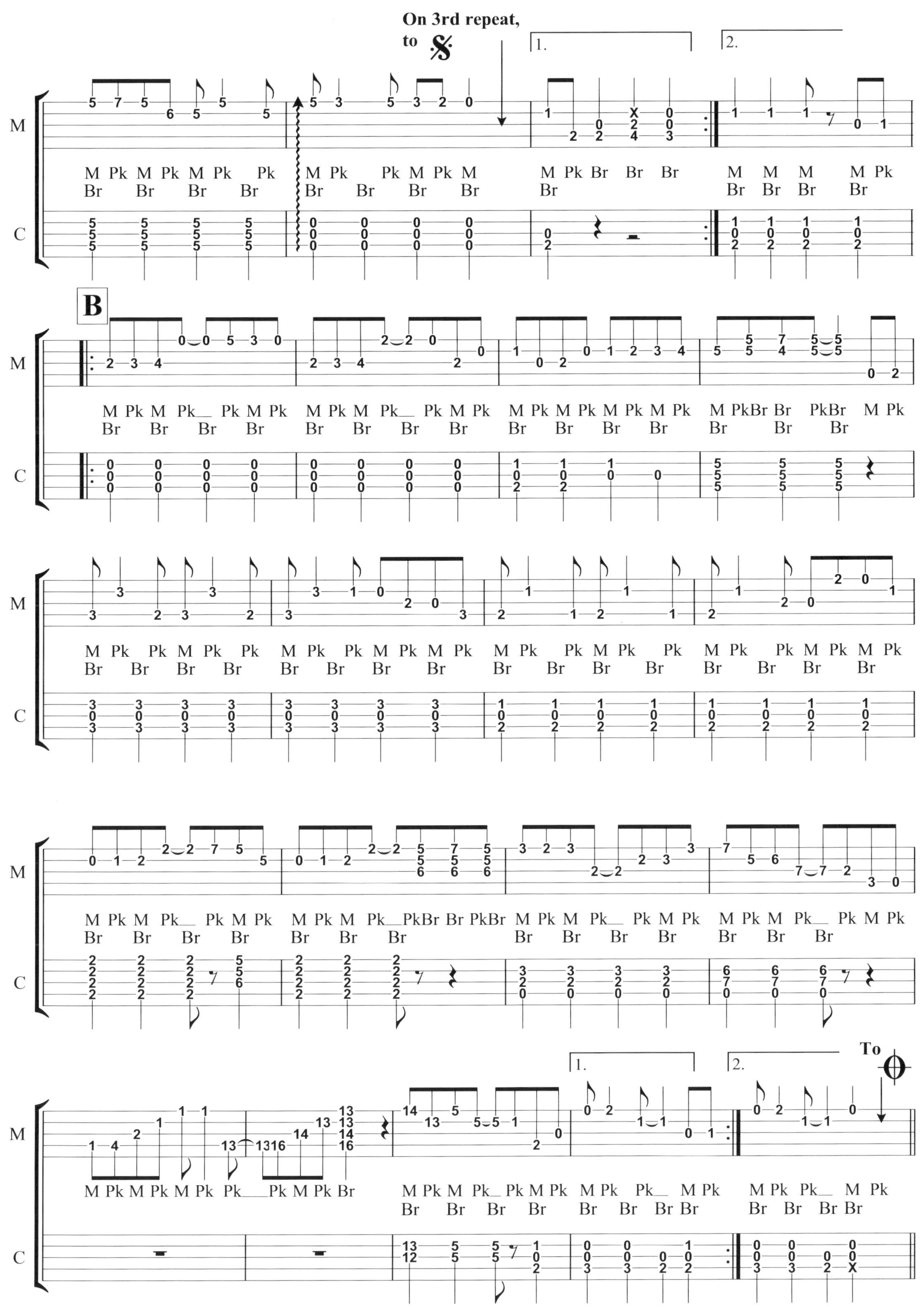
On 3rd repeat,
to
1.
2.
B
M
C
To

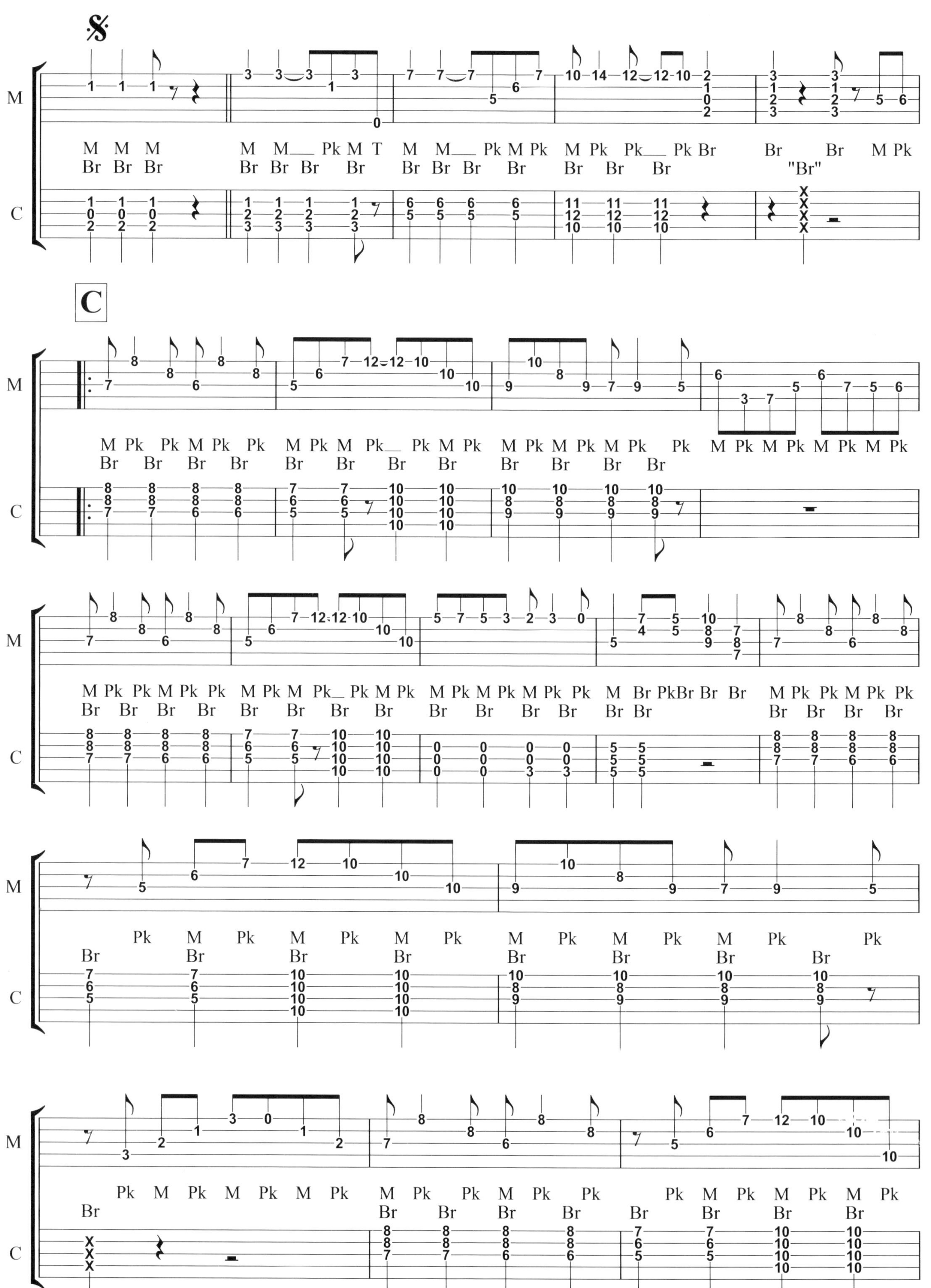
M
C
C
"Br"

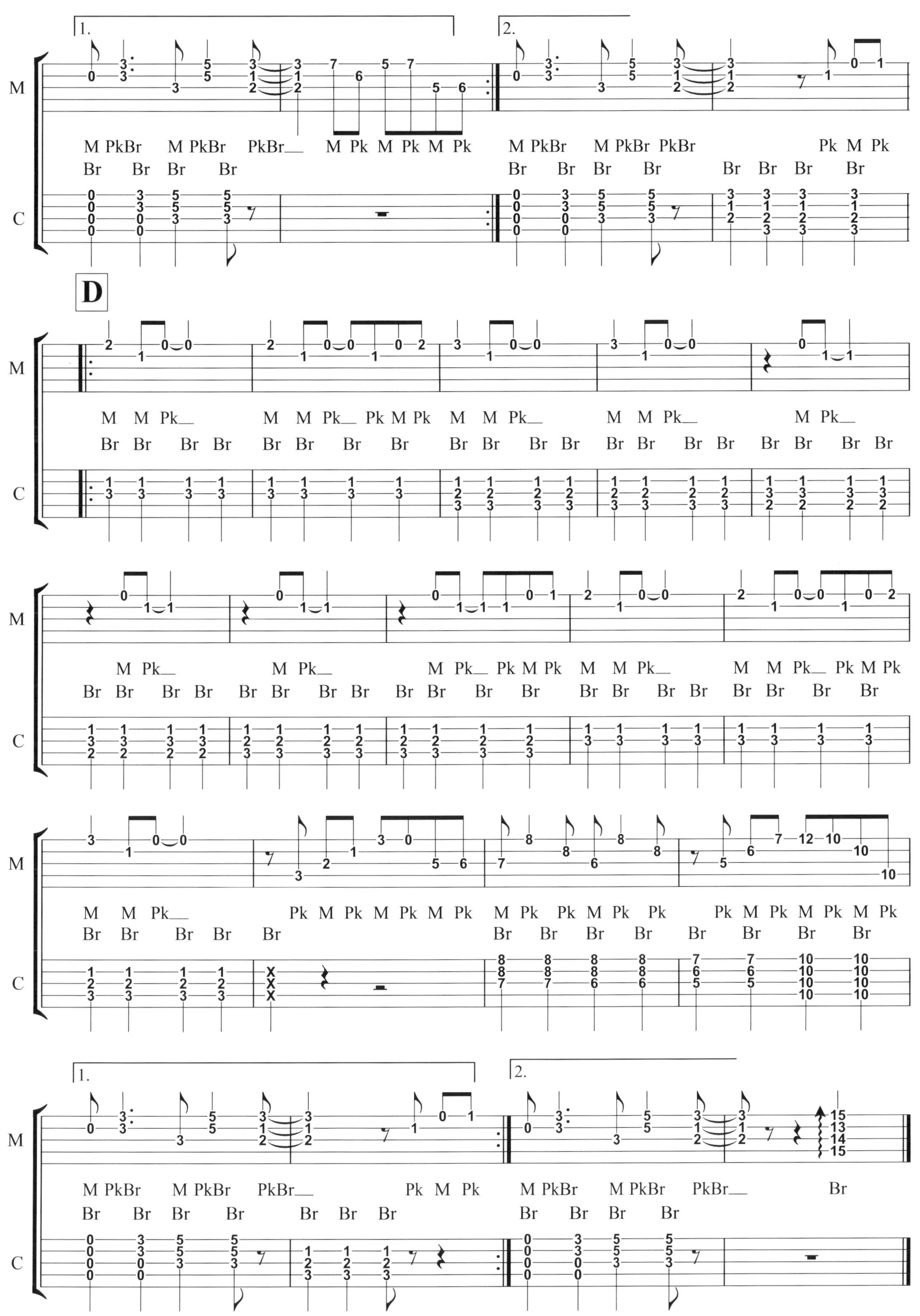
1.
2.
M
C
D
M PkBr M PkBr PkBr M Pk M Pk M Pk
Br Br Br Br
M PkBr M PkBr PkBr Pk M Pk
Br Br Br Br Br Br Br Br
M M Pk M M Pk Pk M Pk M M Pk M M Pk M Pk
Br Br Br Br Br Br Br Br Br Br Br Br Br Br Br Br Br Br Br Br
M Pk M Pk M Pk Pk M Pk M M Pk M M Pk Pk M Pk
Br Br Br Br Br Br Br Br Br Br Br Br Br Br Br Br Br Br Br Br
M M Pk Pk M Pk M Pk M Pk M Pk Pk M Pk Pk Pk M Pk M Pk M Pk
Br Br Br Br Br Br Br Br Br Br Br Br Br
M PkBr M PkBr PkBr Pk M Pk M PkBr M PkBr PkBr Br
Br Br Br Br Br Br Br Br Br Br Br

The Entertainer

Scott Joplin
(arr. Steve Kahn)

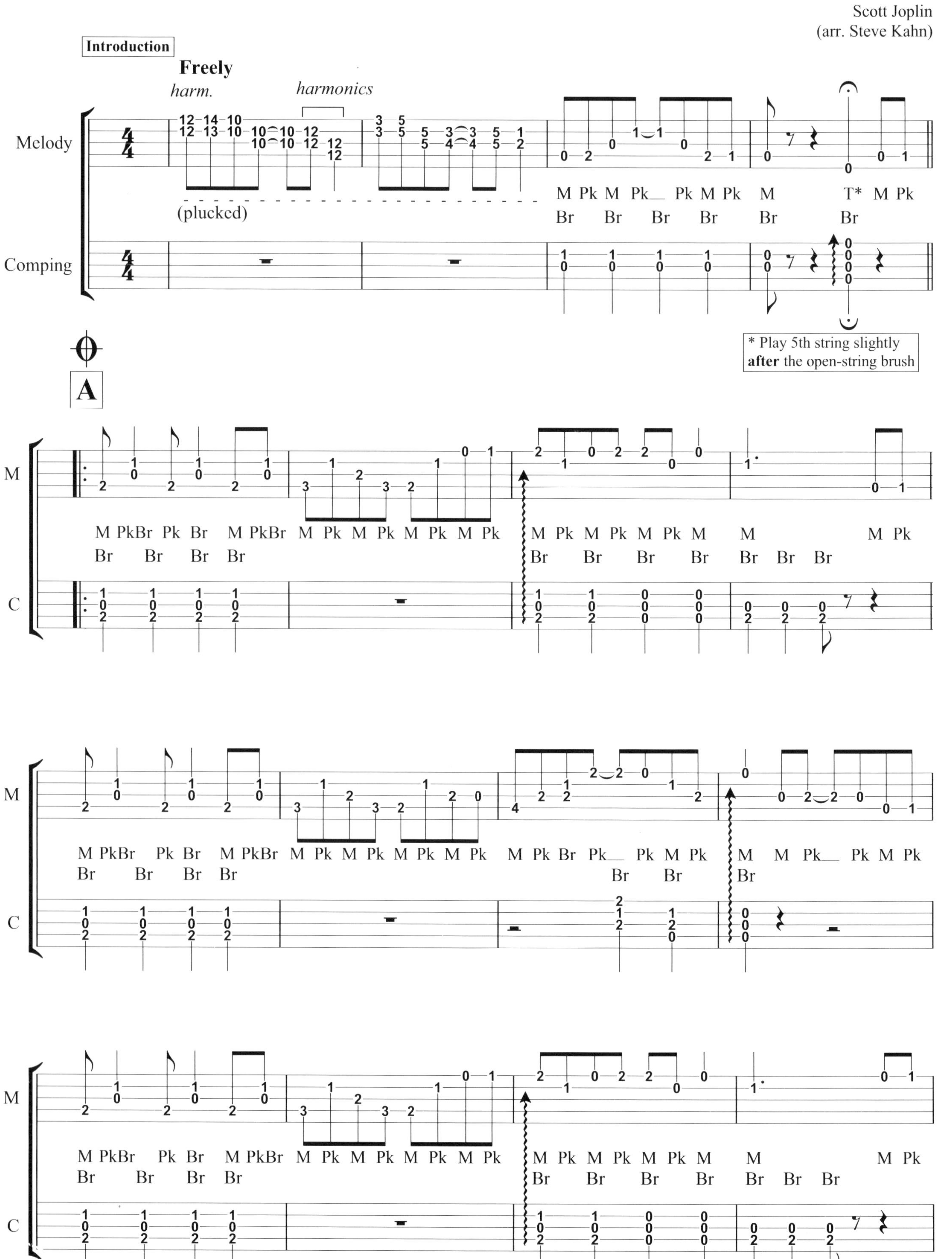

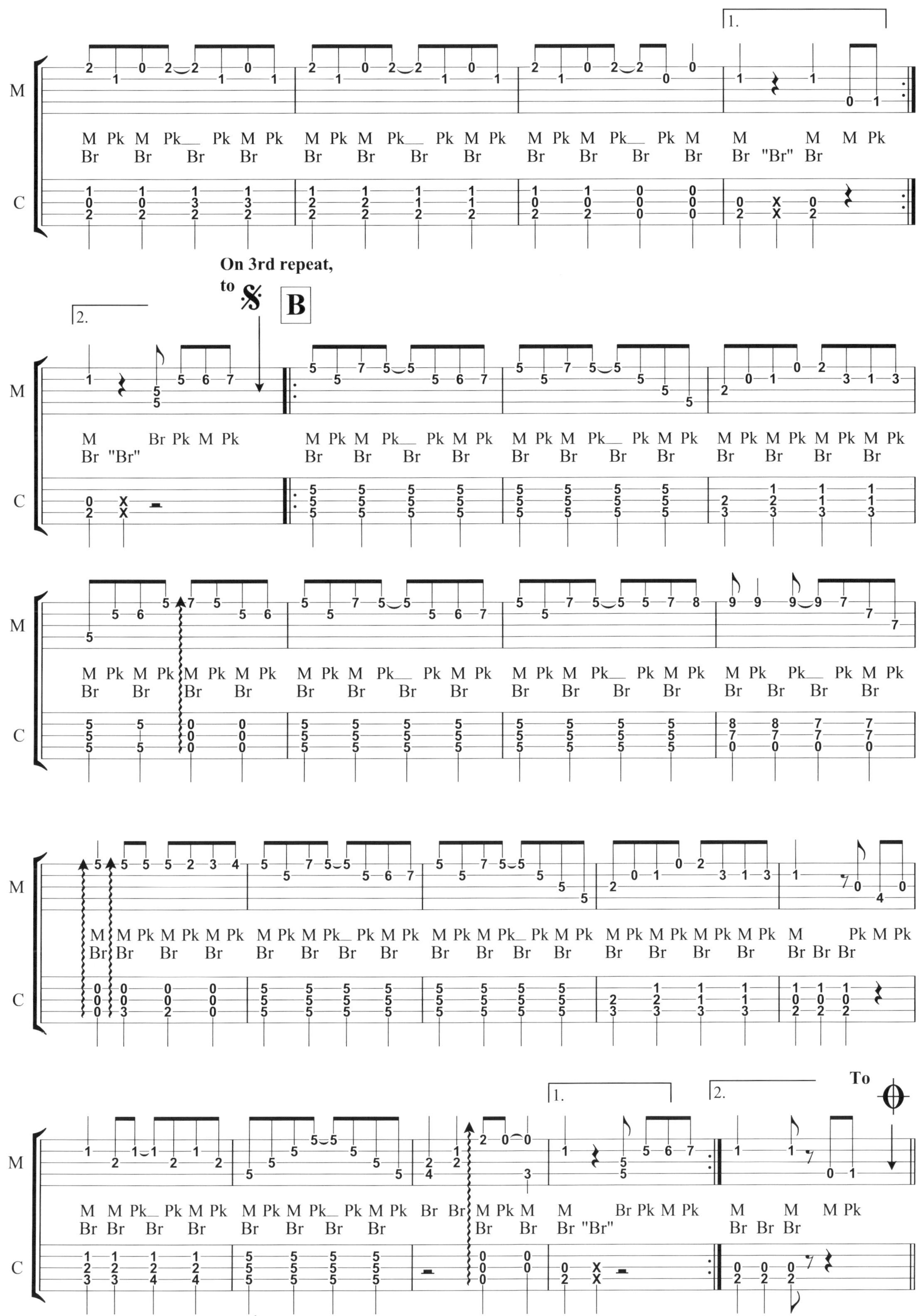

1.
M
C
M Pk M Pk Pk M Pk
Br Br Br Br
"Br"
2.
On 3rd repeat,
to
B
To

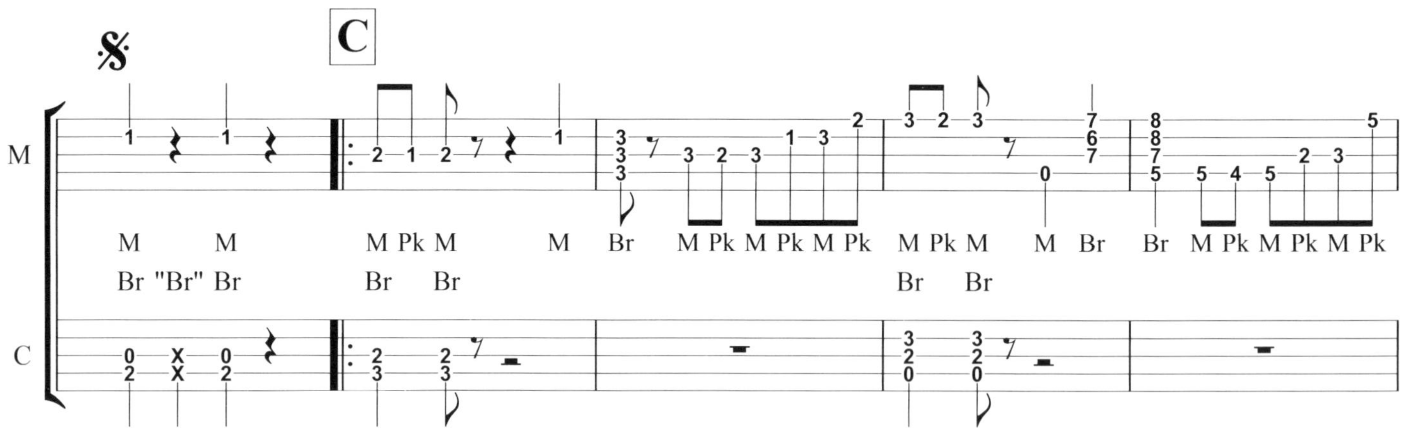
C
M
C
M M
Br "Br" Br
M Pk M M Br M Pk M Pk M Pk M Pk M Pk M M Br Br M Pk M Pk M Pk
Br Br Br Br

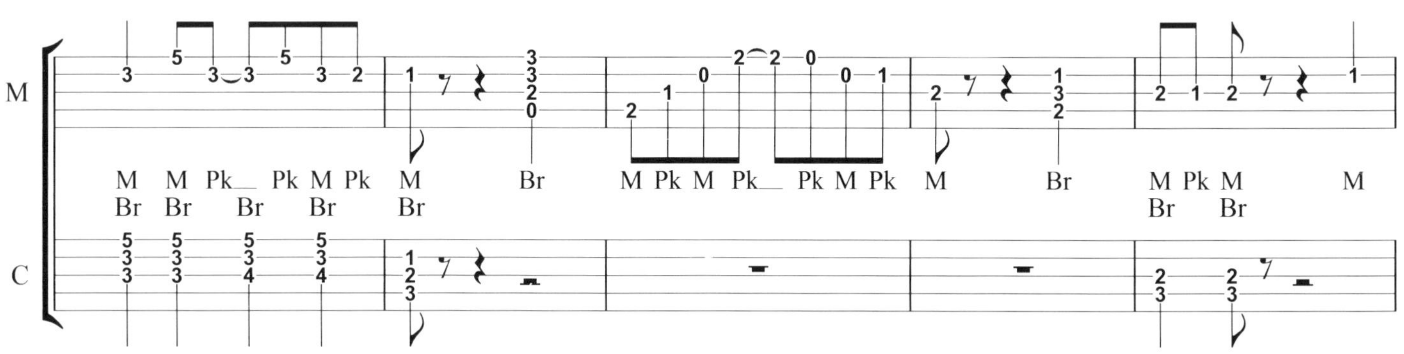
M
C
M M Pk Pk M Pk M Br M Pk M Pk Pk M Pk M Br M Pk M M
Br Br Br Br Br Br Br

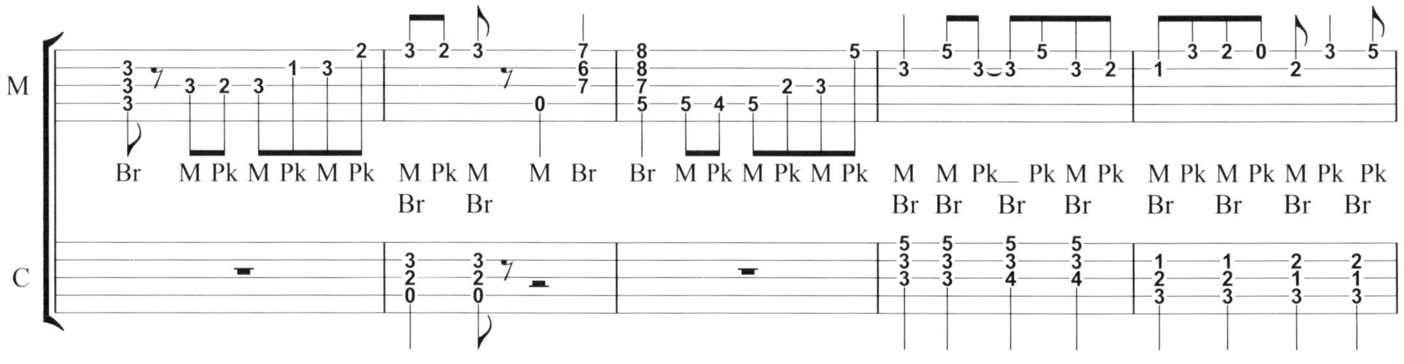
M
C
Br M Pk M Pk M Pk M Pk M M Br Br M Pk M Pk M Pk M M Pk Pk M Pk M Pk M Pk M Pk M Pk Pk
Br Br Br Br Br Br Br Br Br Br

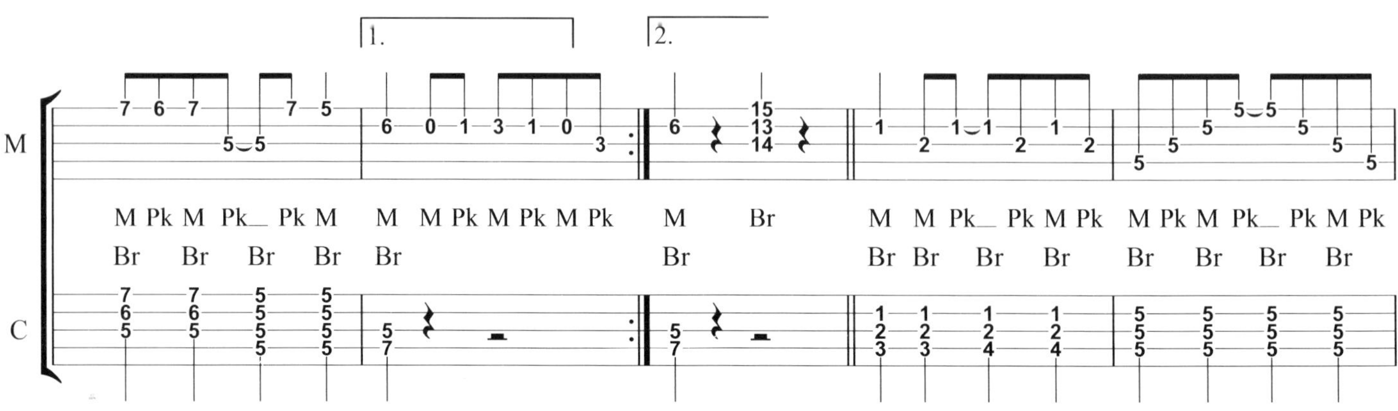
1.
2.
M
C
M Pk M Pk Pk M M M Pk M Pk M Pk M Br M M Pk Pk M Pk M Pk M Pk Pk M Pk
Br Br Br Br Br Br Br Br Br Br Br Br Br Br

D

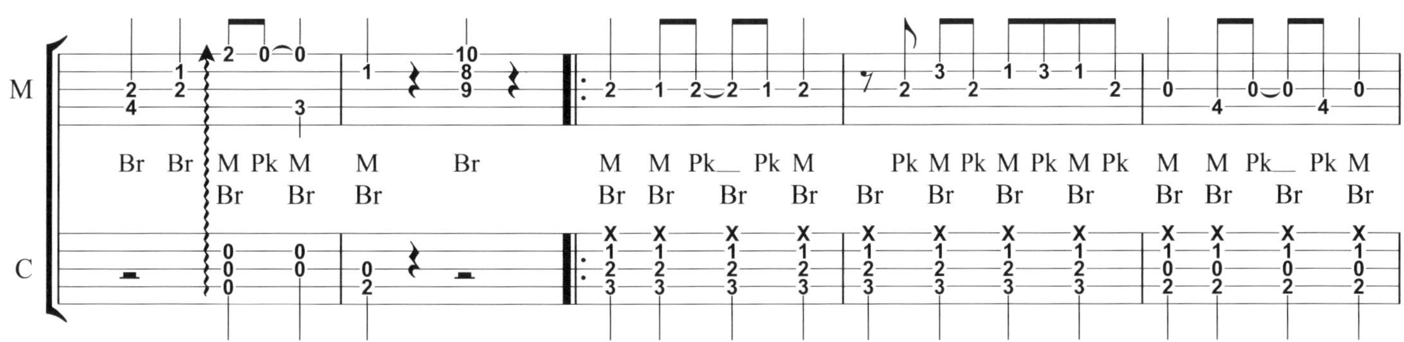
M
C

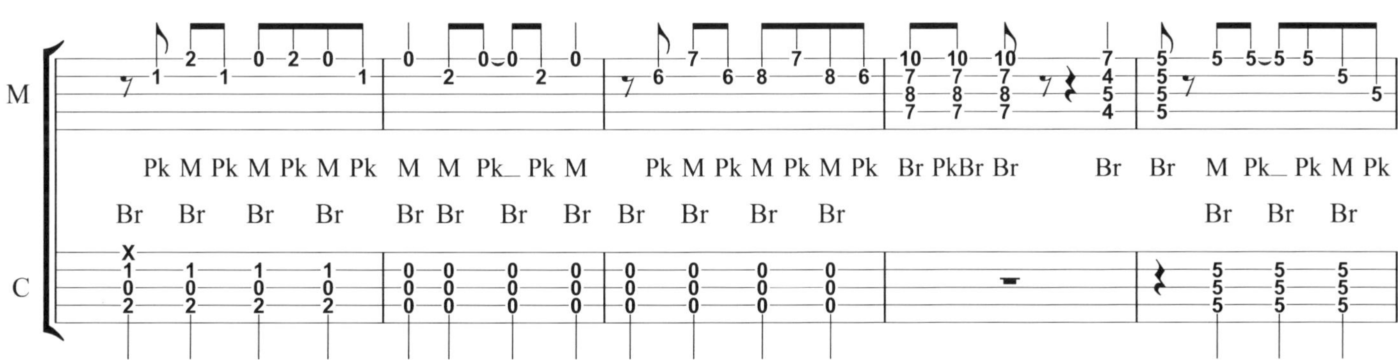
M
C

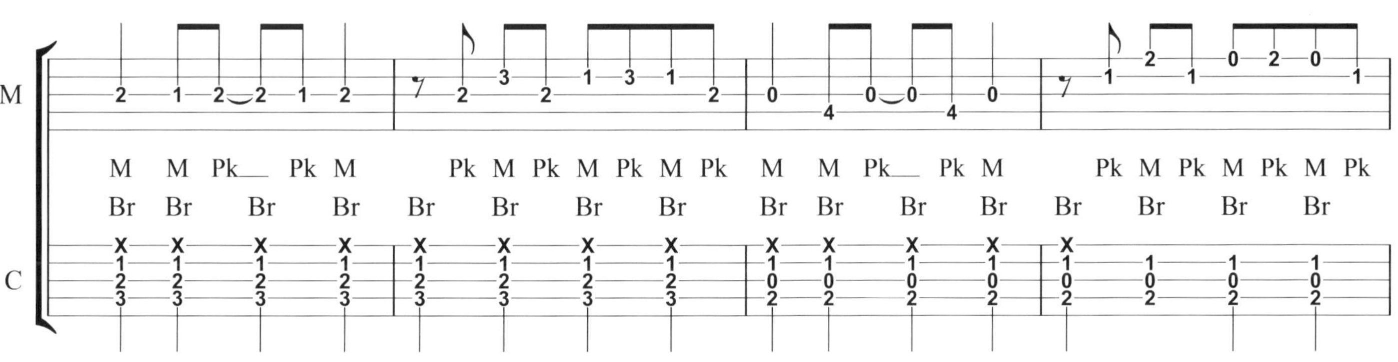
M
C

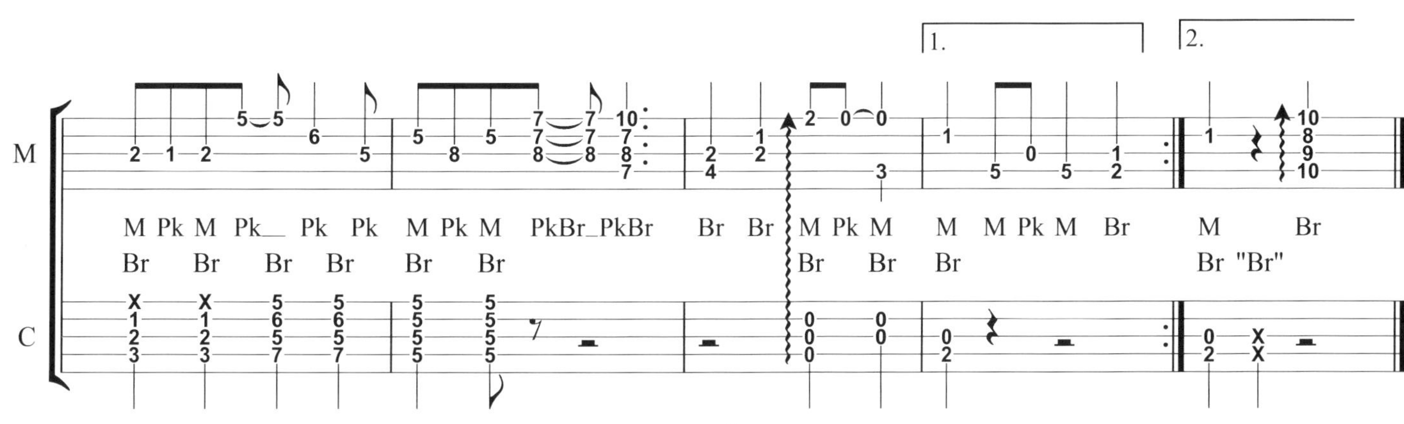
1.
2.
M
C

Gladiolus Rag

Scott Joplin
(arr. Steve Kahn)

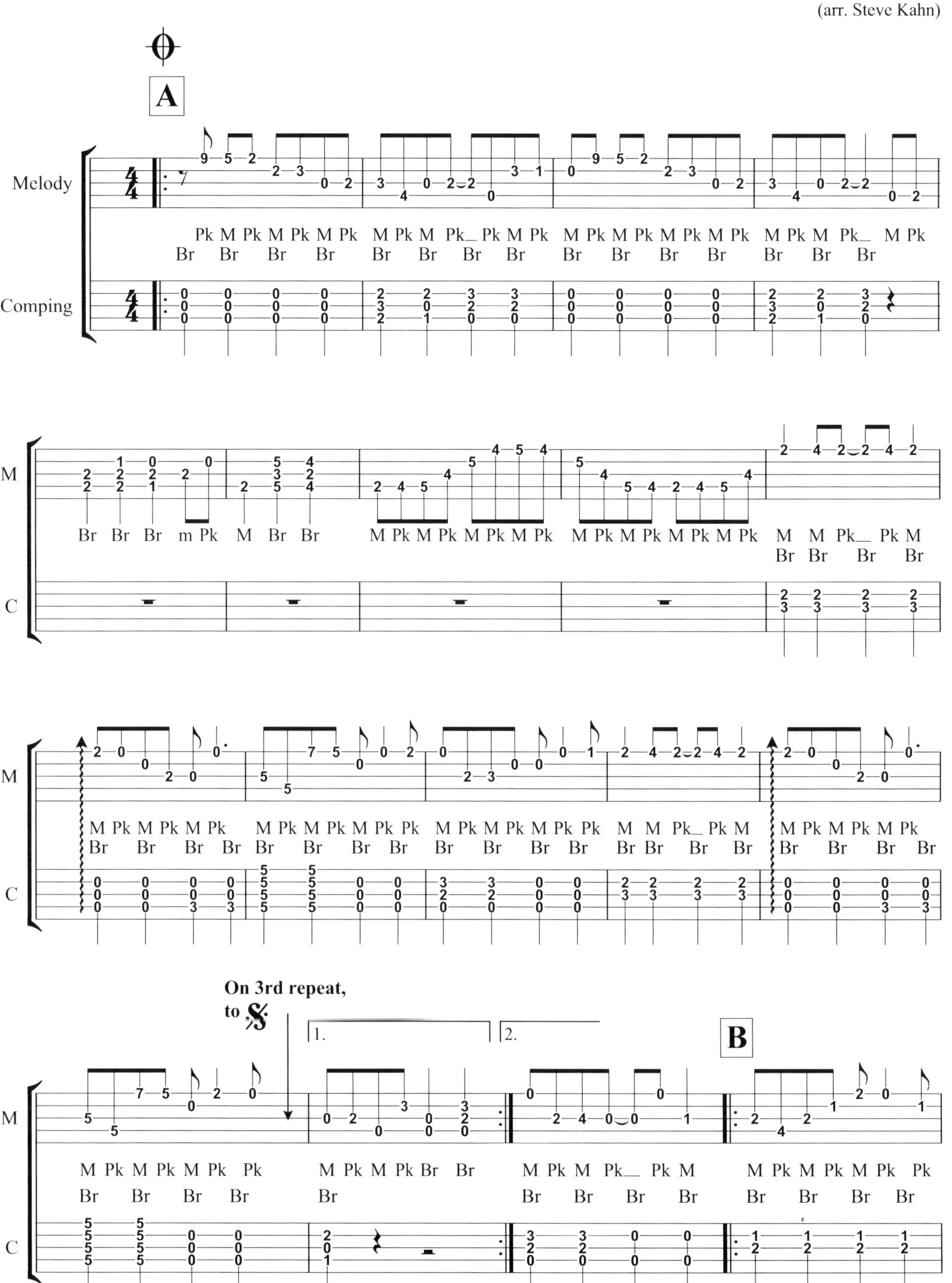

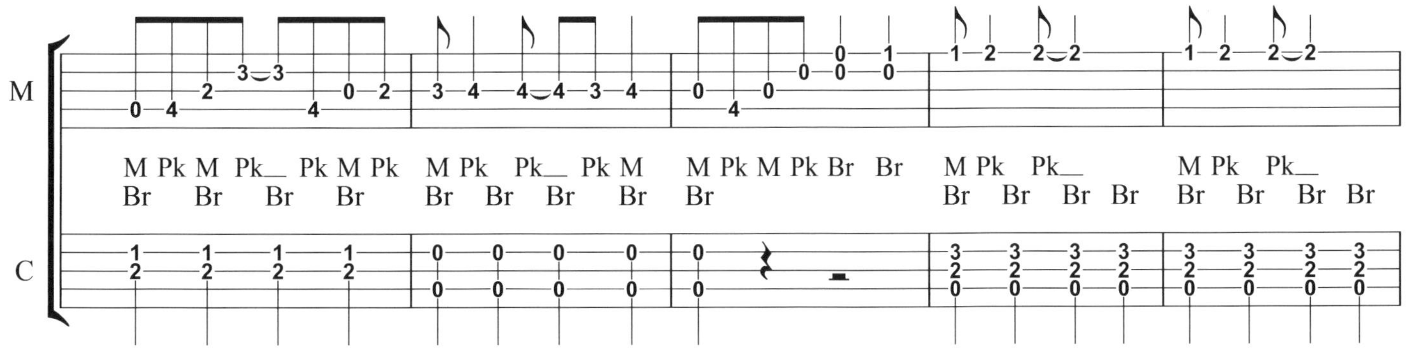

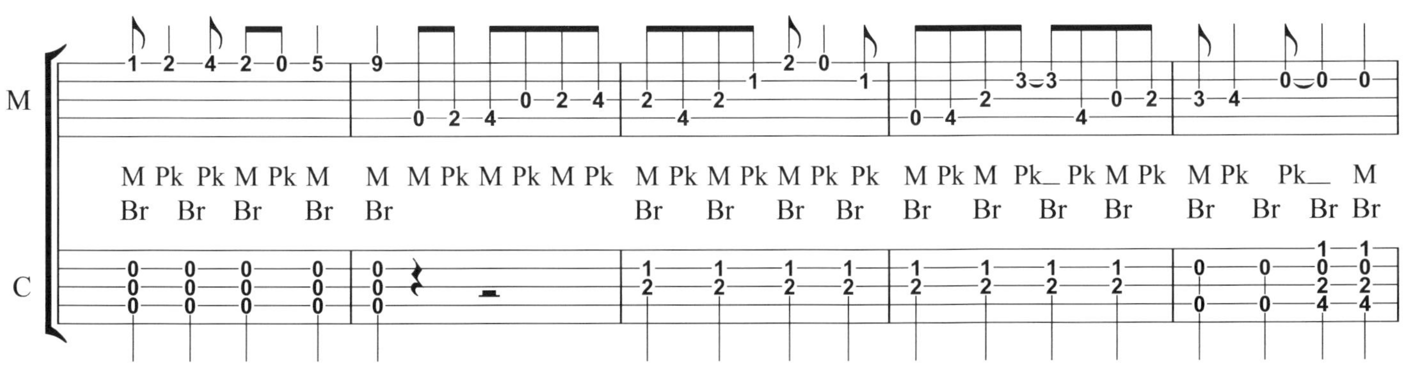

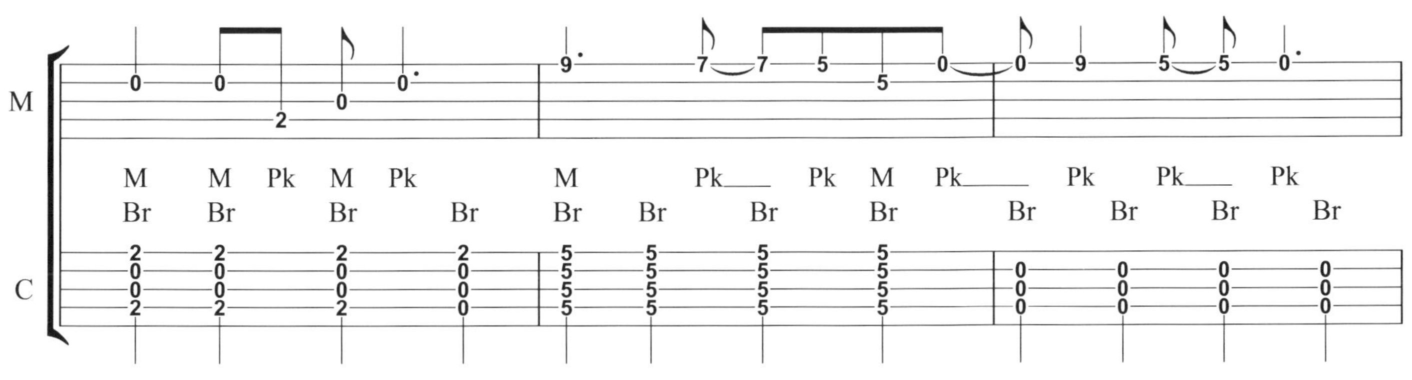

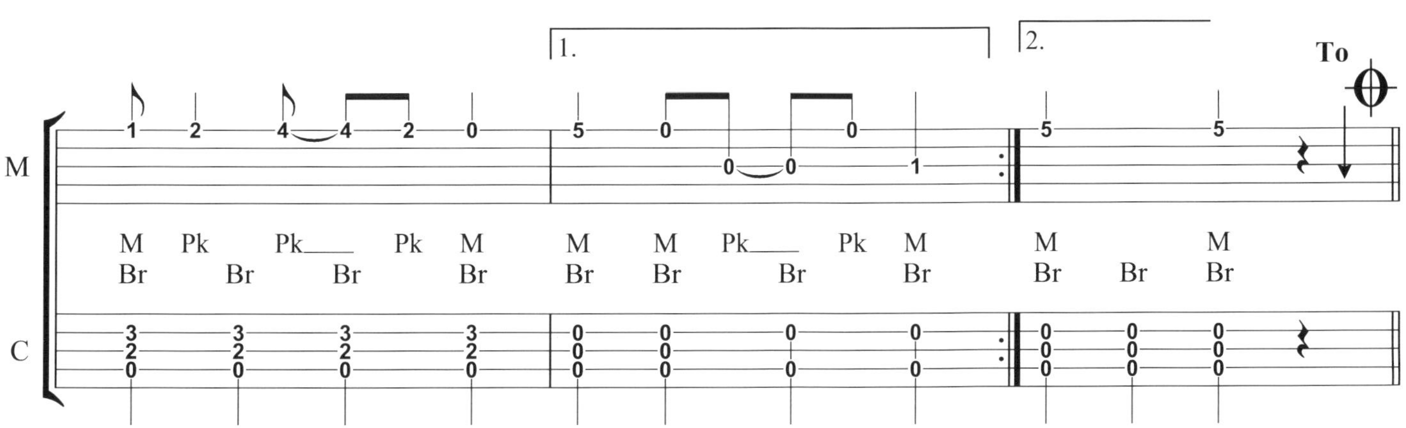
To

C

M
C
M Pk M Pk M Pk M
Br Br Br Br
M Pk Pk M M Pk
Br Br Br Br Br
M Pk M Pk M
M Pk Pk Pk M Pk
Br Br Br Br

1.
2.
M
C
M Pk Pk Pk M
Br Br Br Br
M Pk Pk Pk M
Br Br Br Br
M M Pk Pk M Pk
Br Br Br Br
M Pk M M
Br Br Br Br

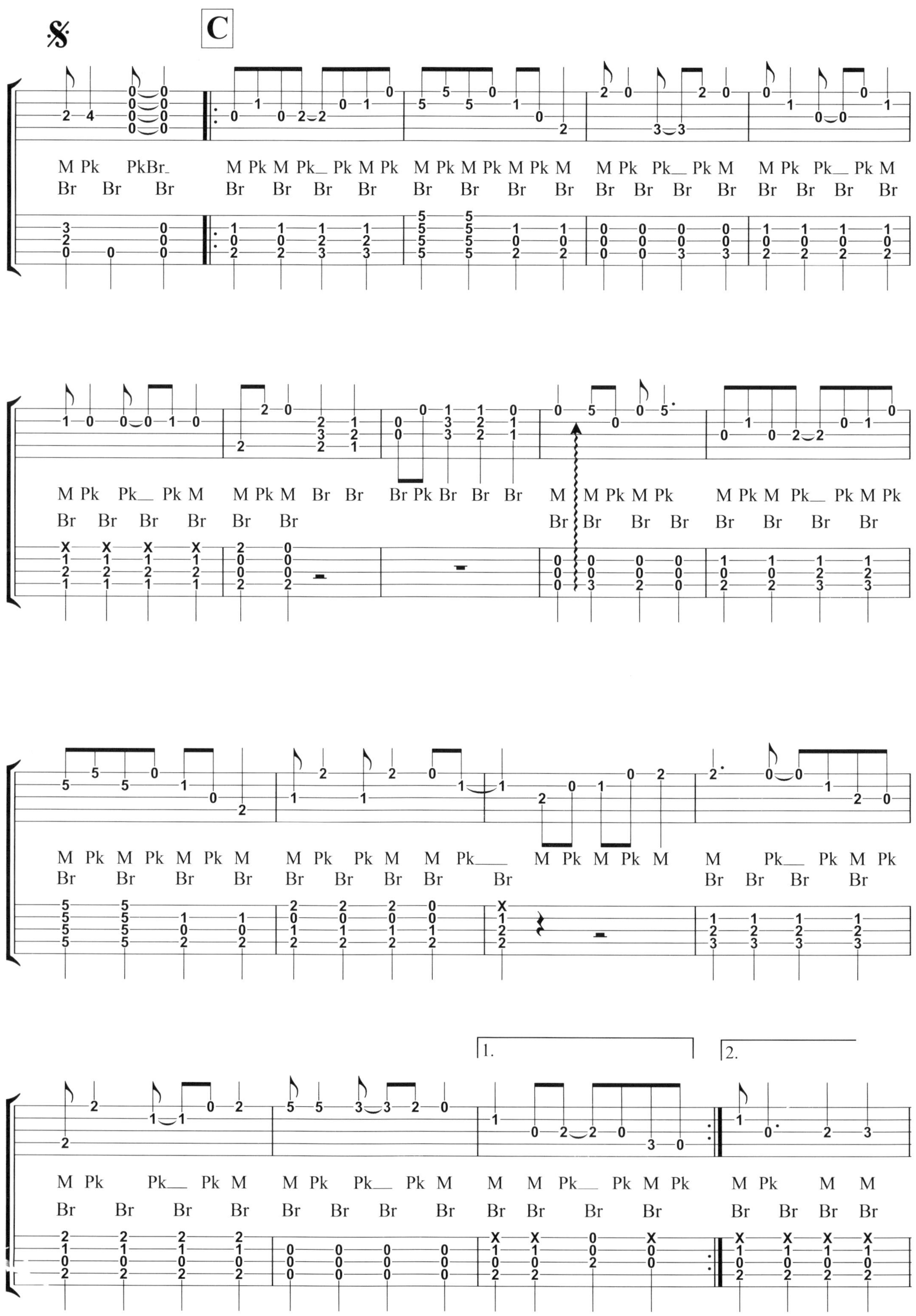

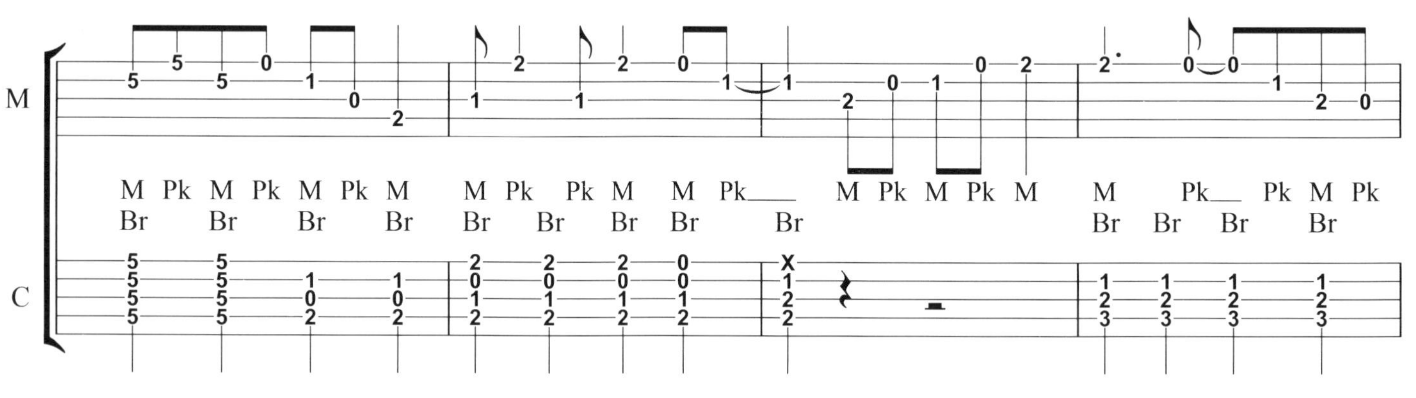

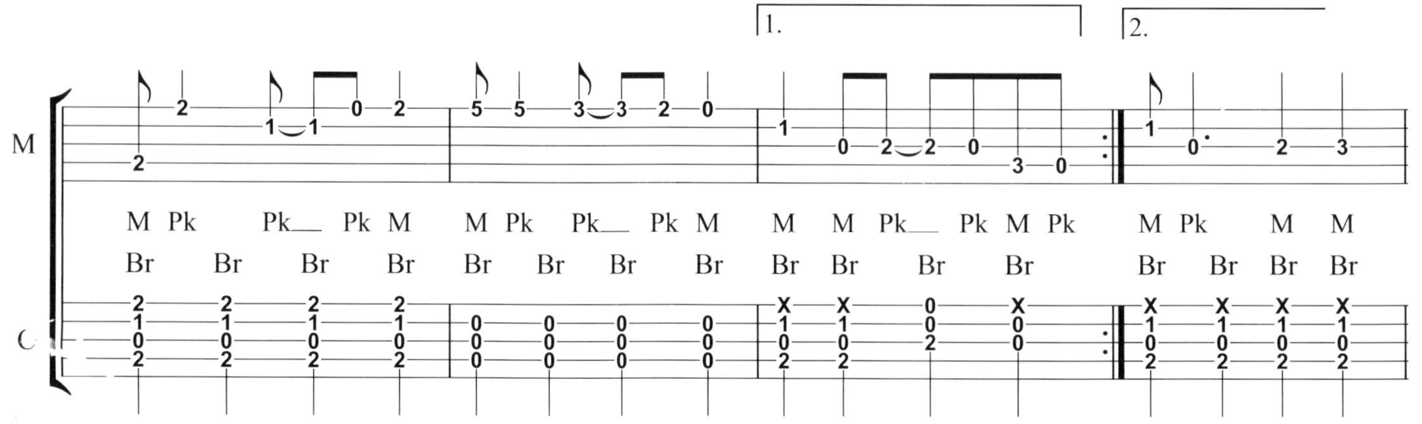

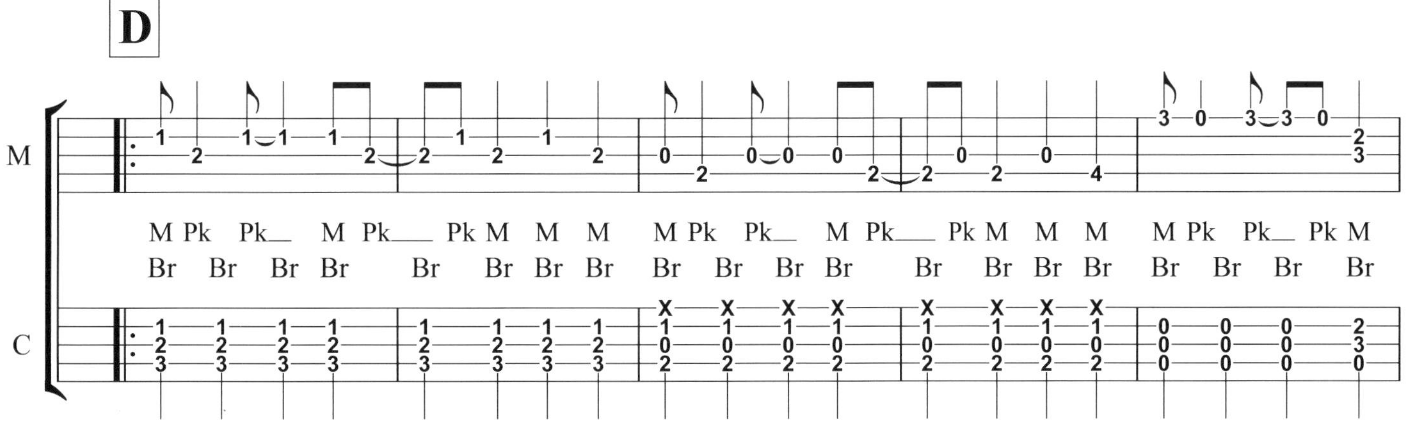
D
M
C
M Pk Pk M Pk Pk M M M M Pk Pk M Pk Pk M M M M Pk Pk Pk M
Br Br Br Br Br Br Br Br Br Br Br Br Br Br Br Br Br Br Br Br

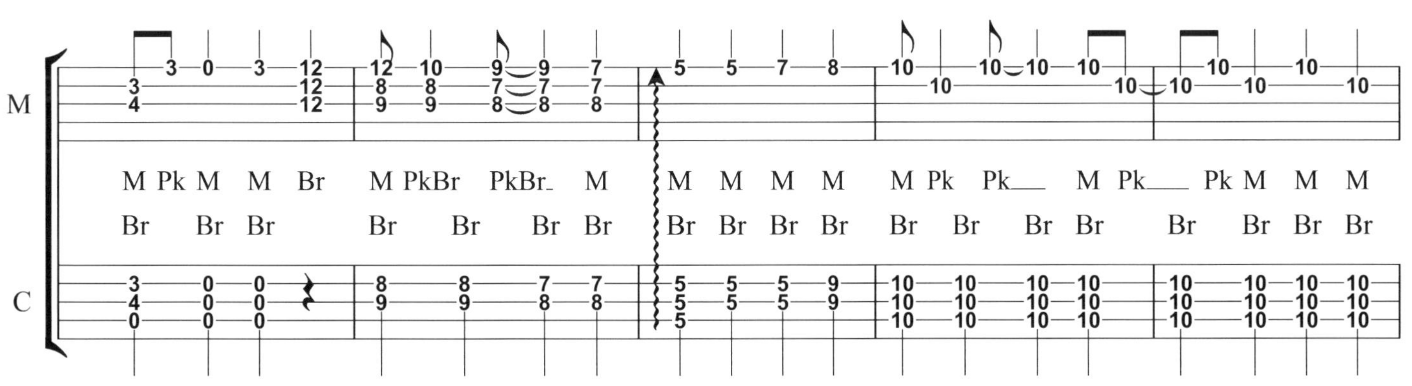
M
C
M Pk M M Br M PkBr PkBr M M M M M M Pk Pk M Pk Pk M M M
Br Br Br Br Br Br Br Br Br Br Br Br Br Br Br Br Br Br Br Br Br

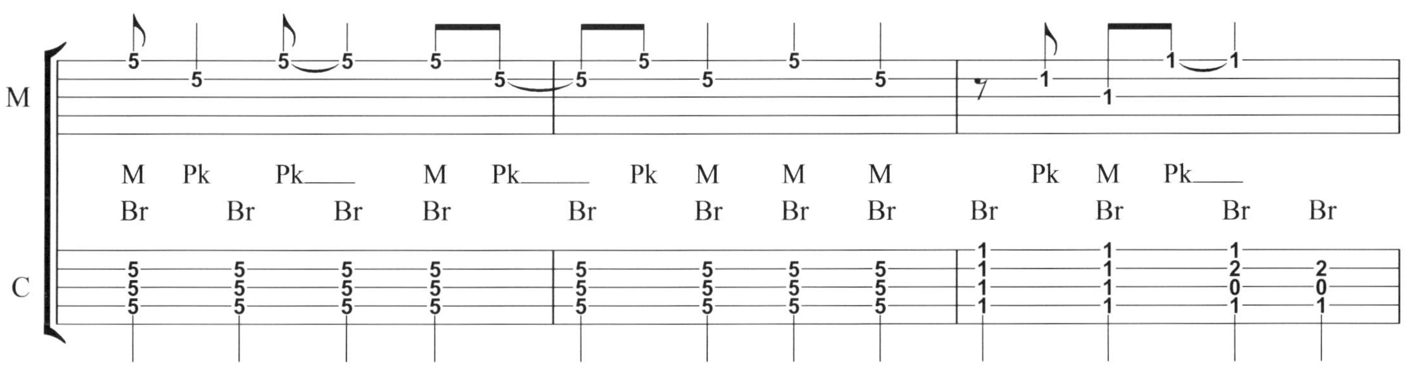
M
C
M Pk Pk M Pk Pk M M M Pk M Pk
Br Br Br Br Br Br Br Br Br Br Br Br

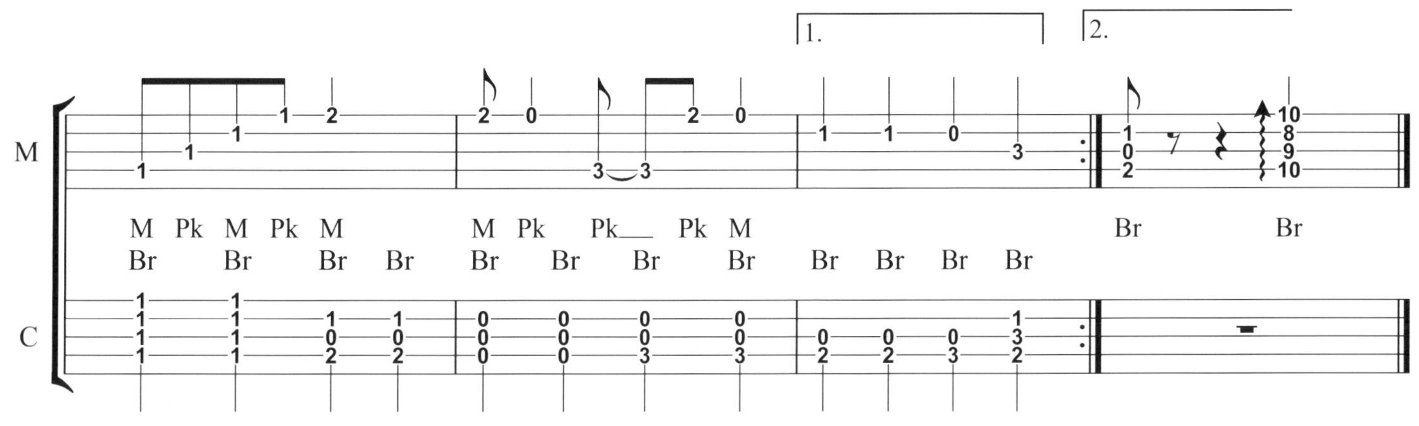
1.
2.
M
C
M Pk M Pk M M Pk Pk Pk M Br Br
Br Br Br Br Br Br Br Br Br Br Br Br

Maple Leaf Rag

Scott Joplin
(arr. Steve Kahn)

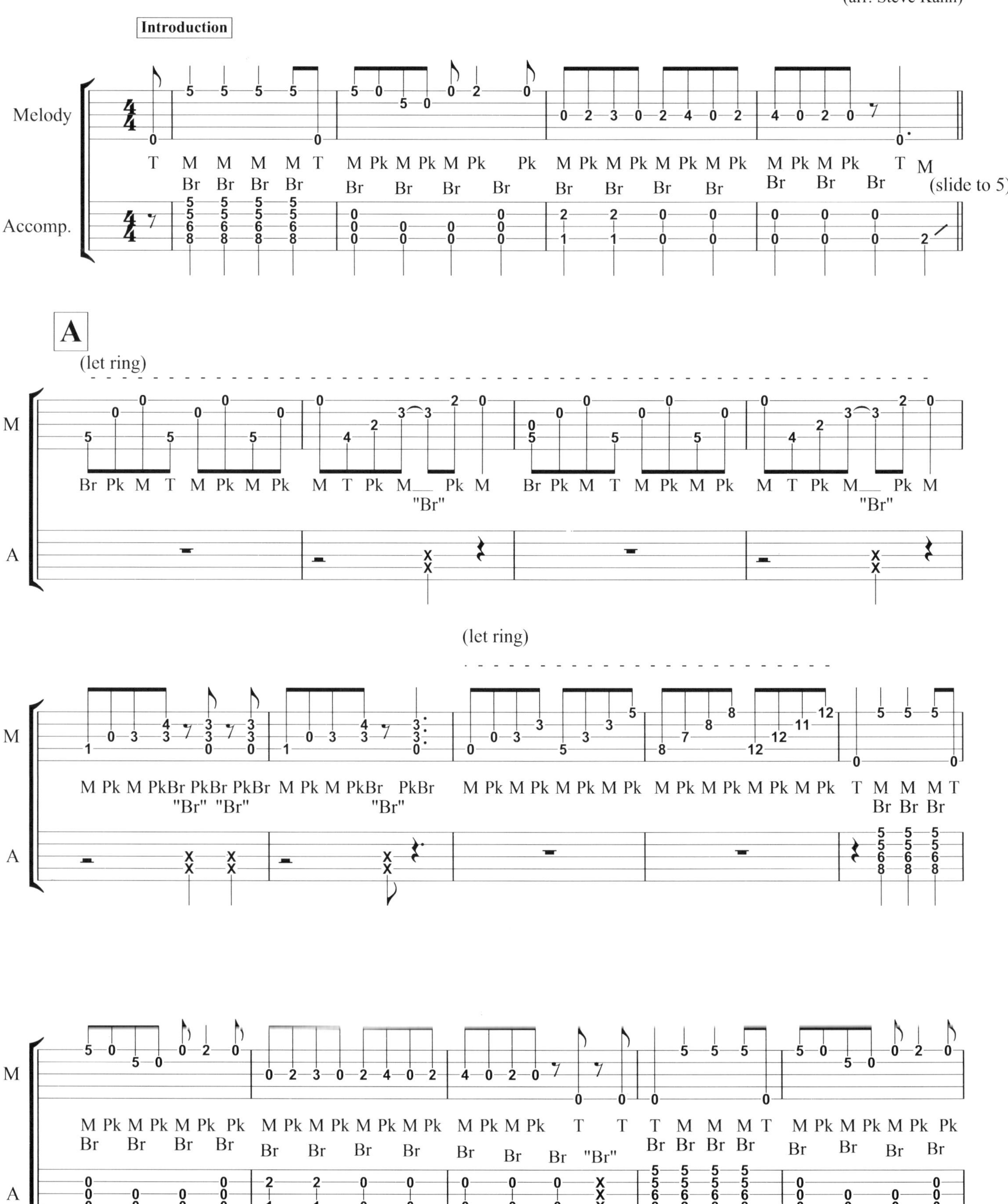

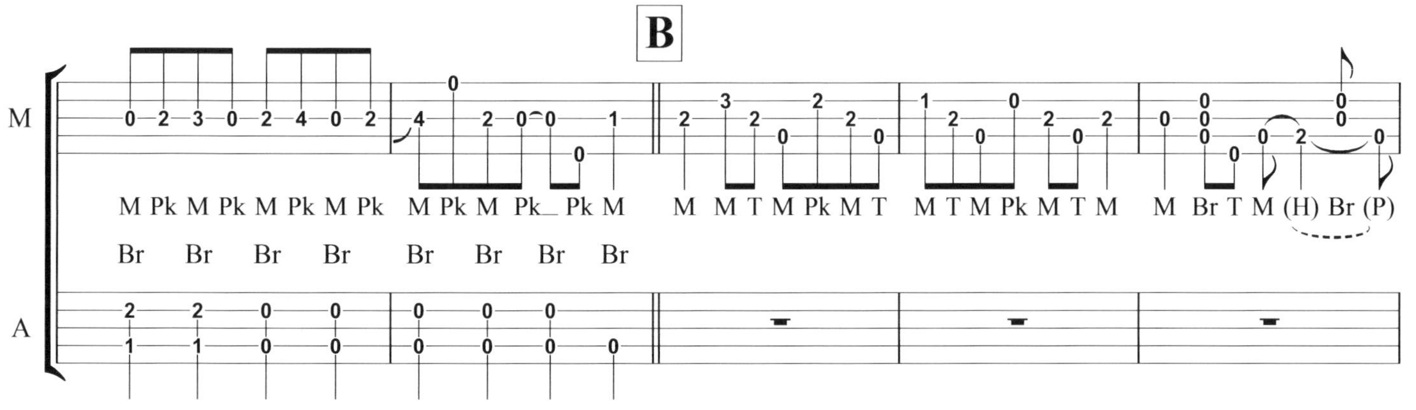

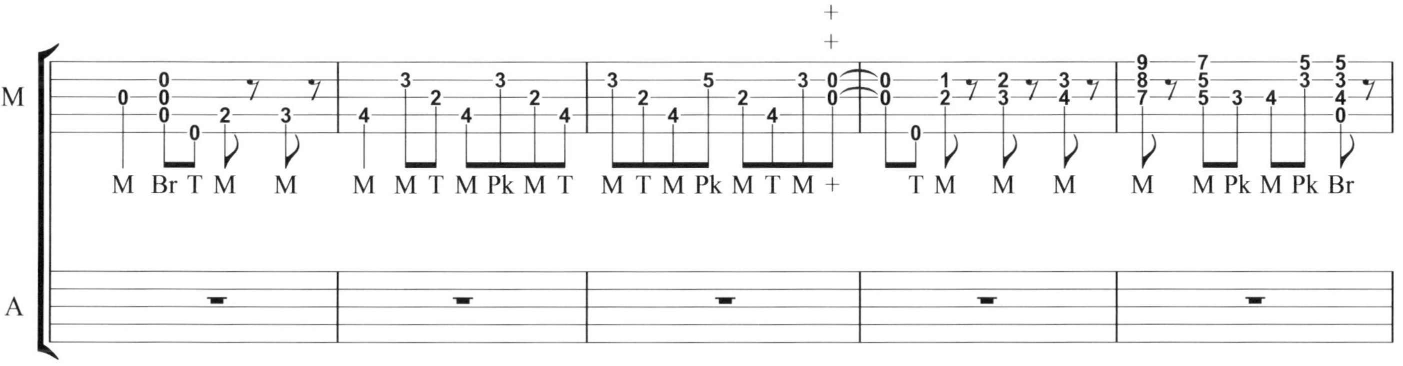

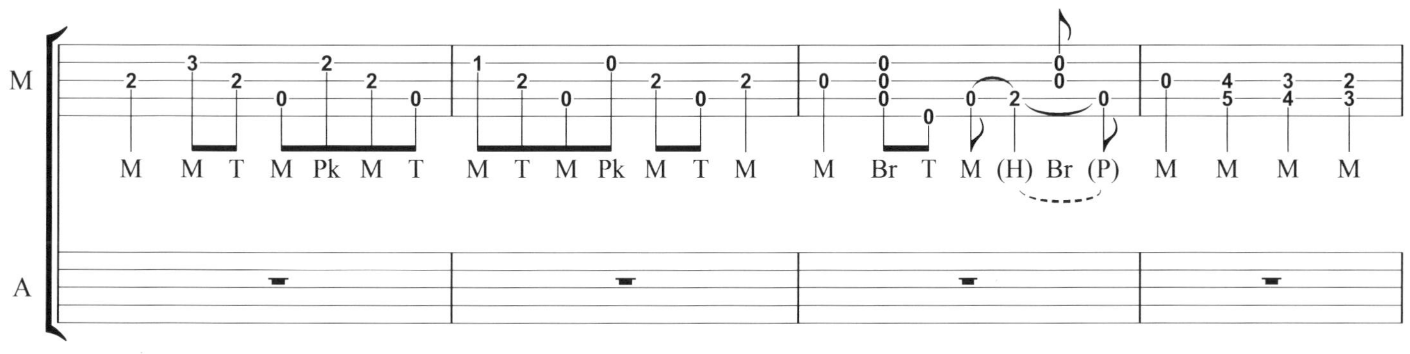

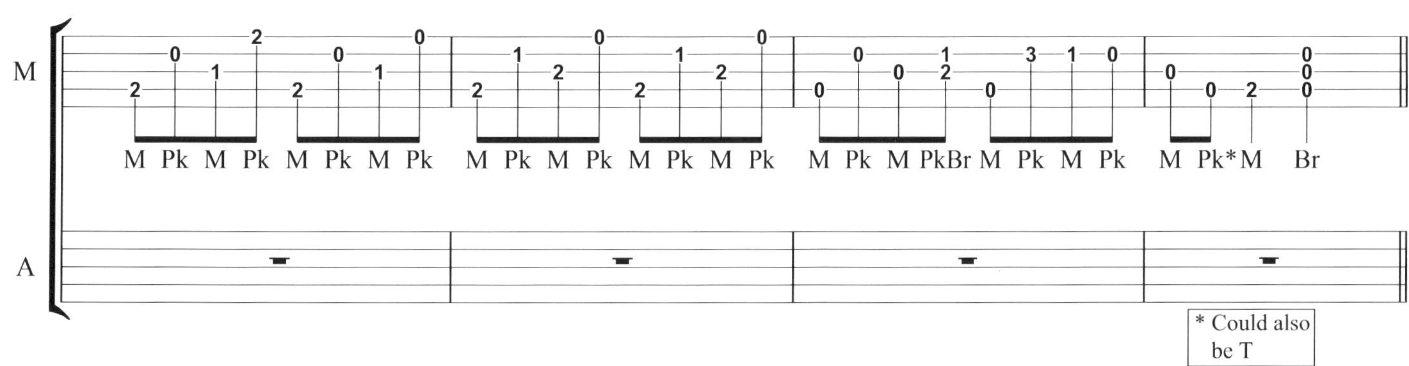

* Could also be T

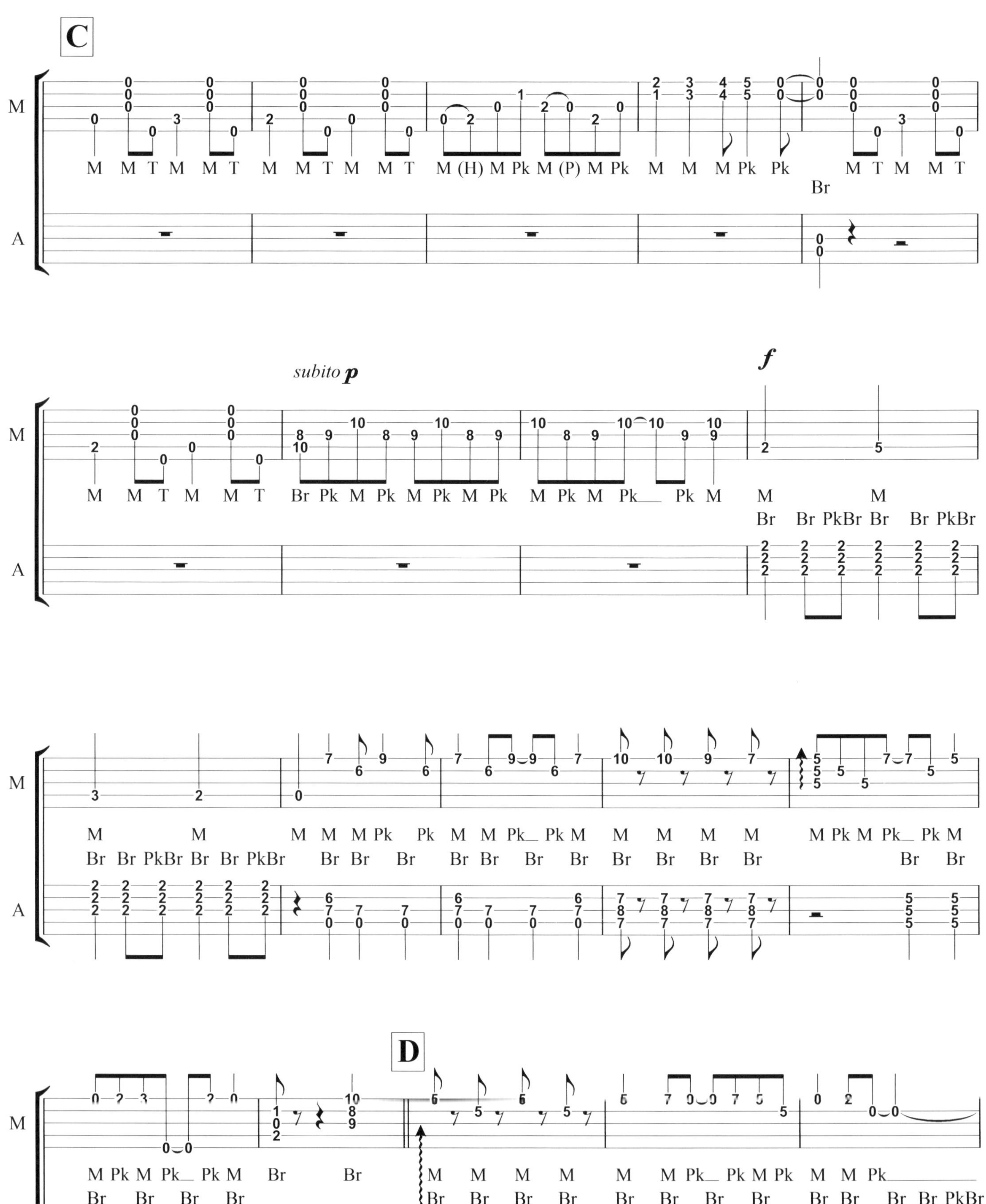
C
subito p
f
D
M
A

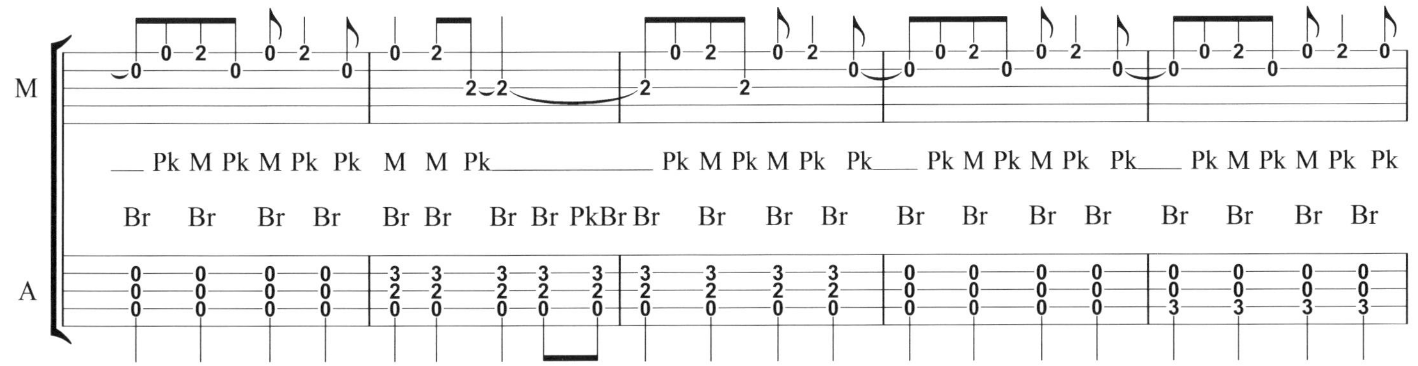

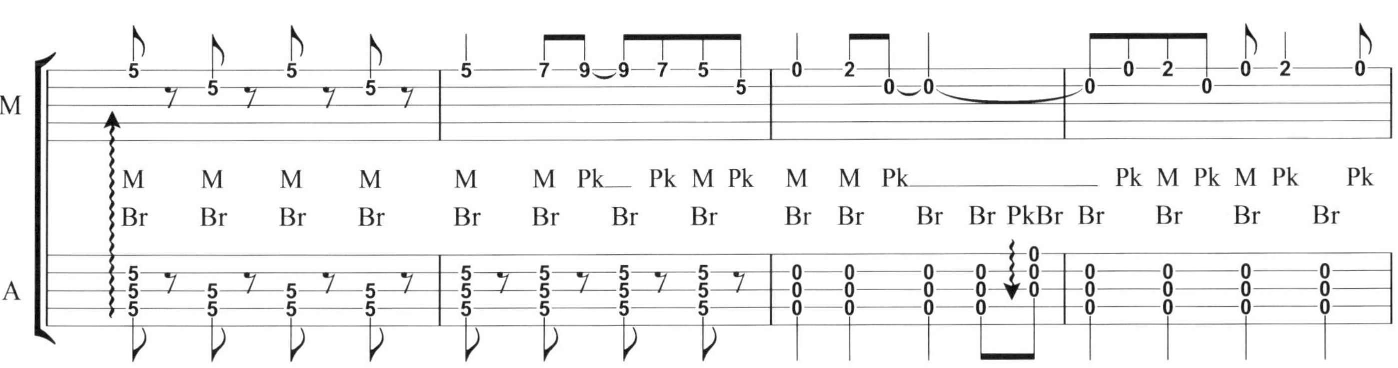

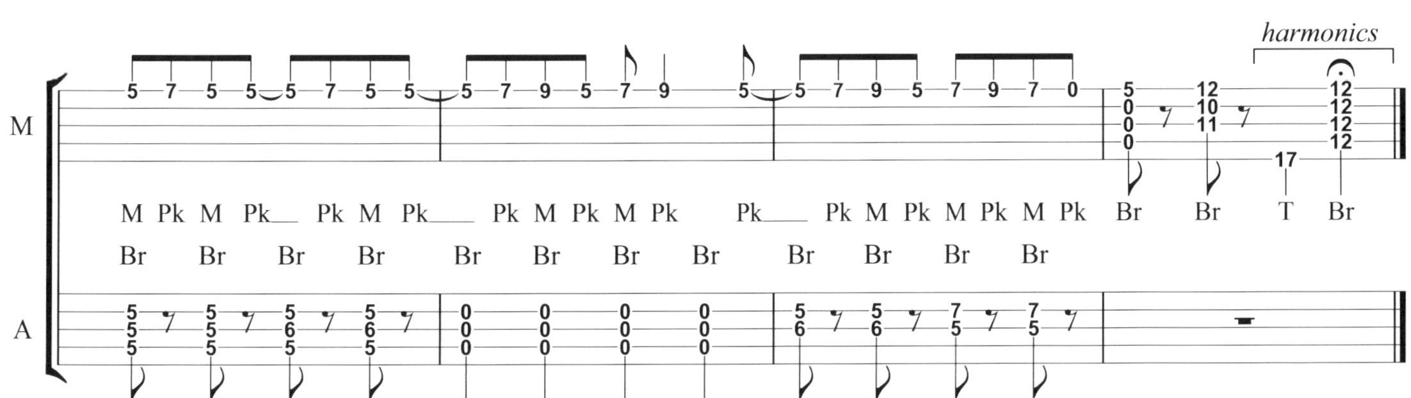
harmonics

Pineapple Rag

Scott Joplin
(arr. Steve Kahn)

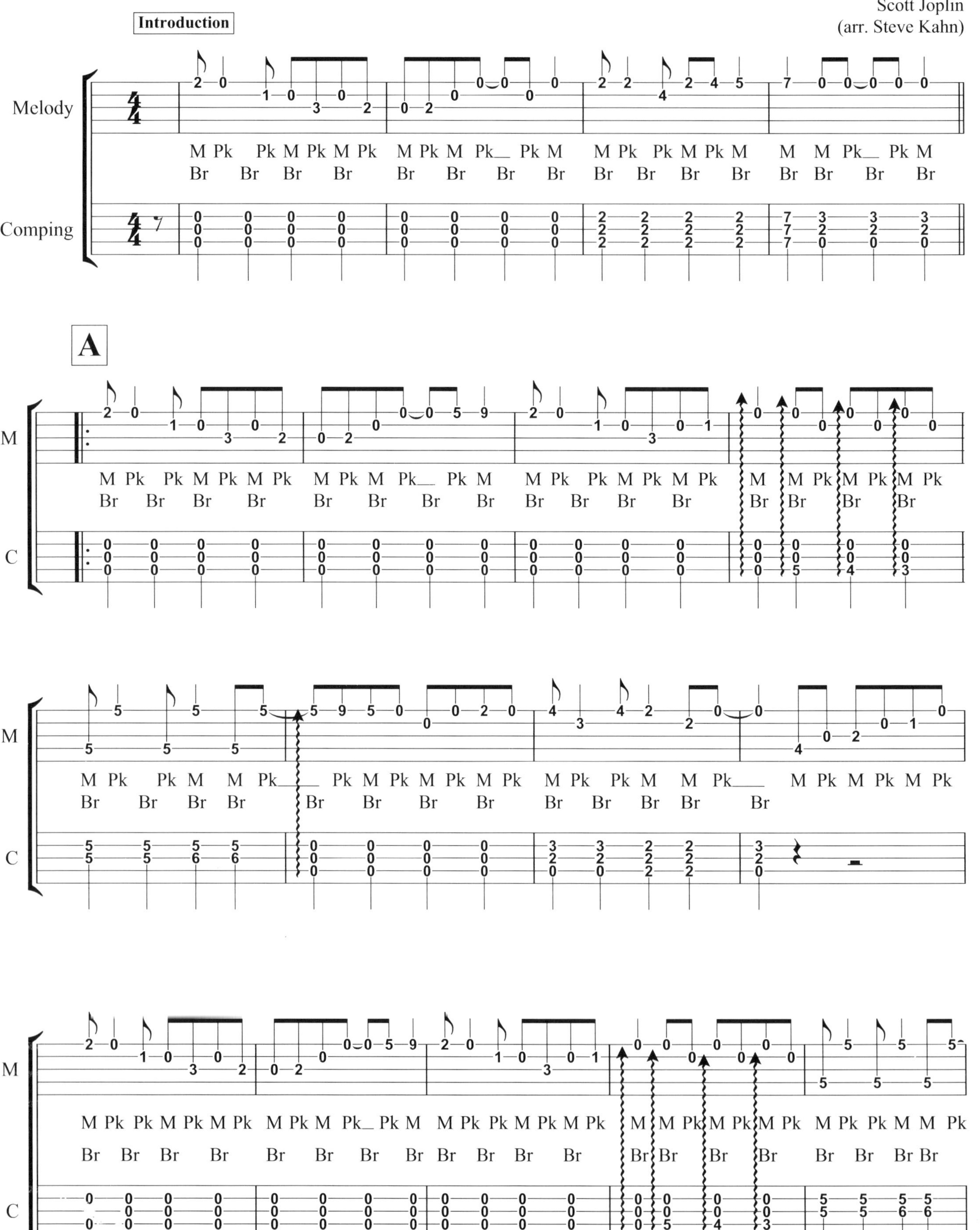

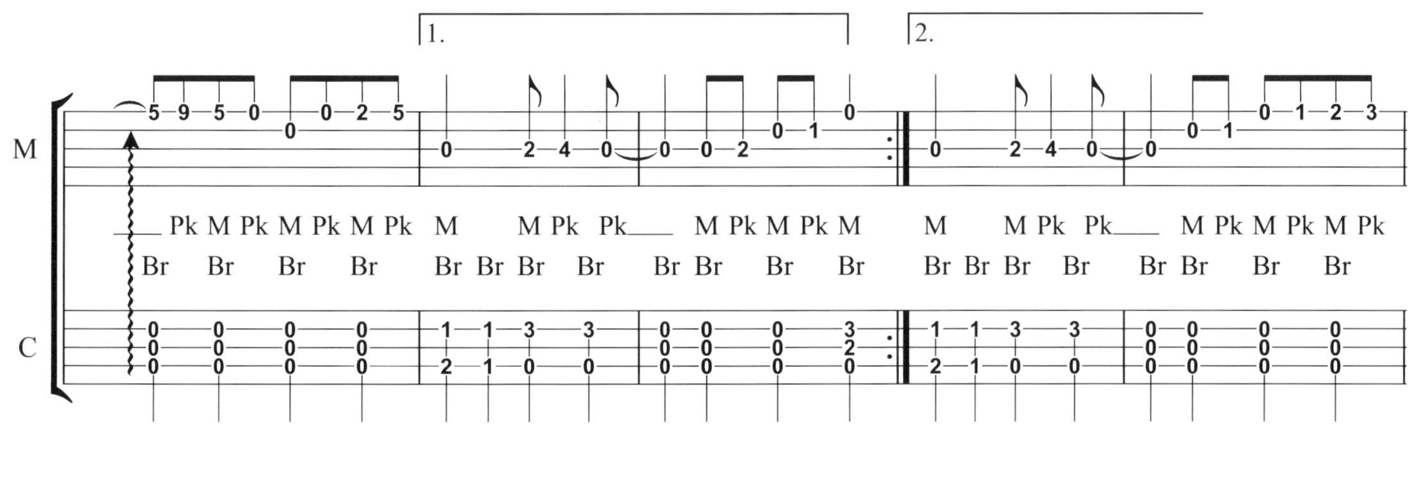

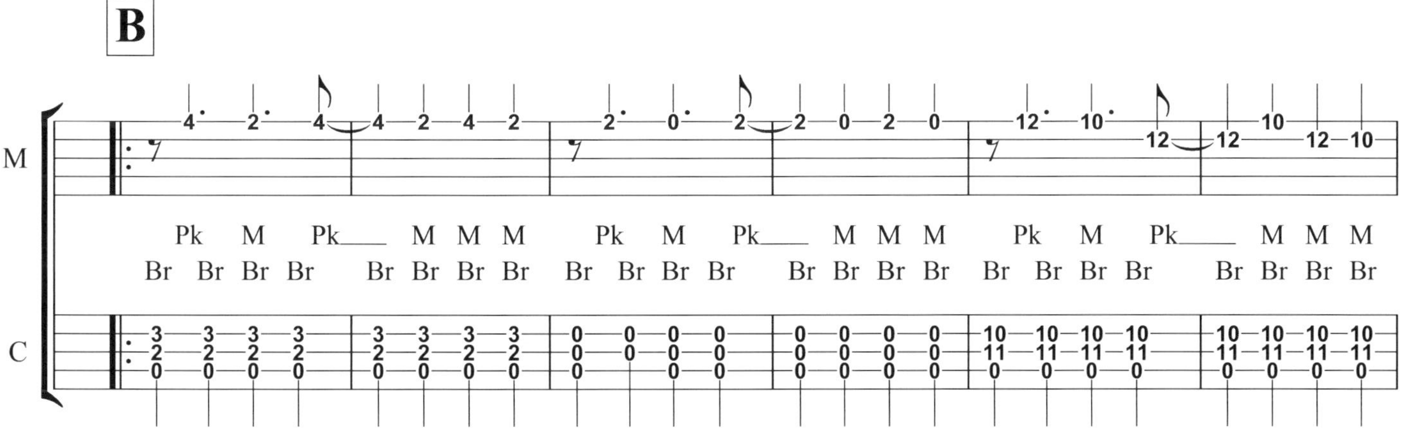

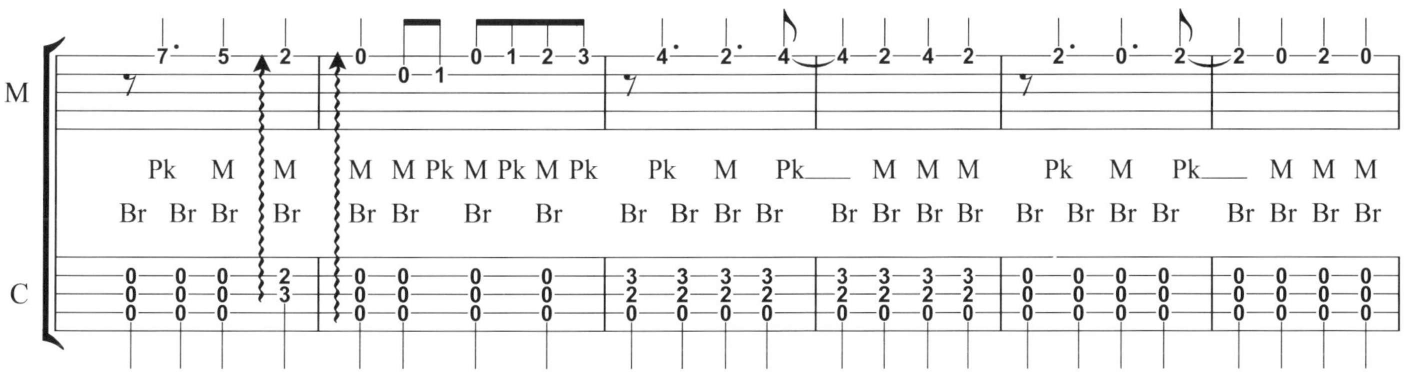

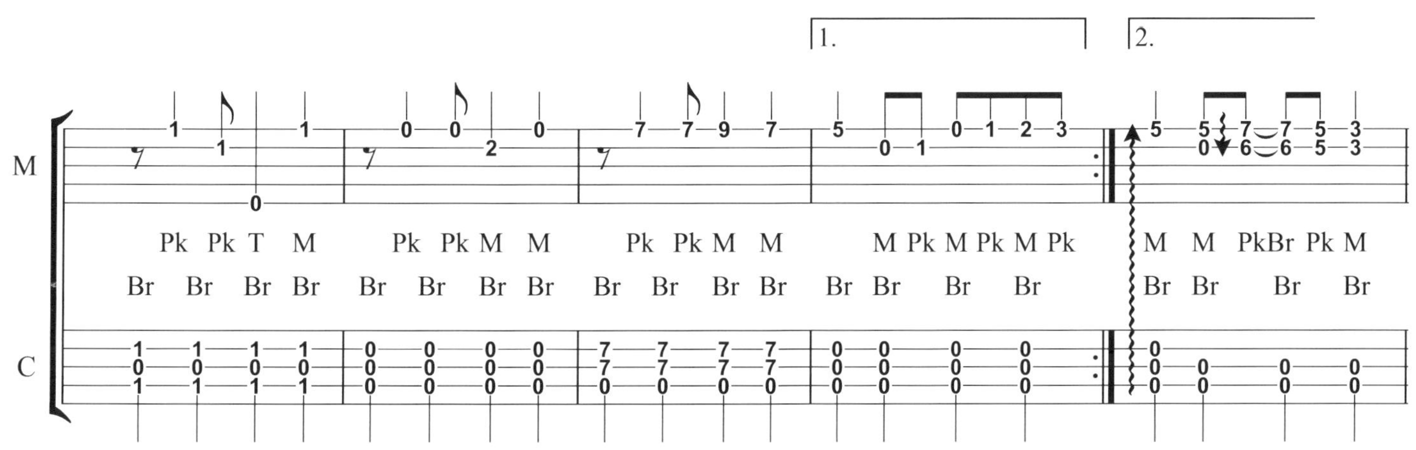

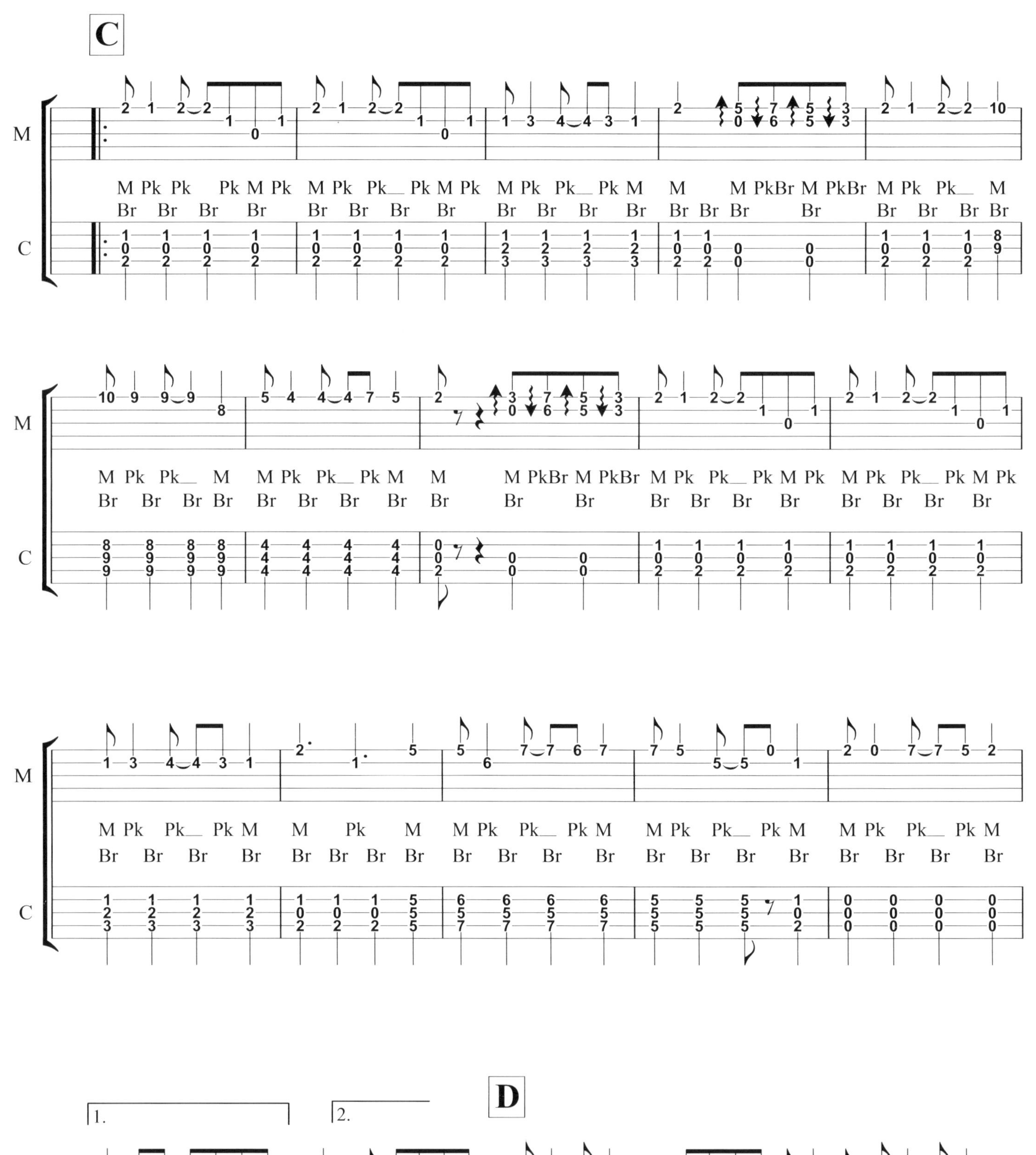

1.
2.

D

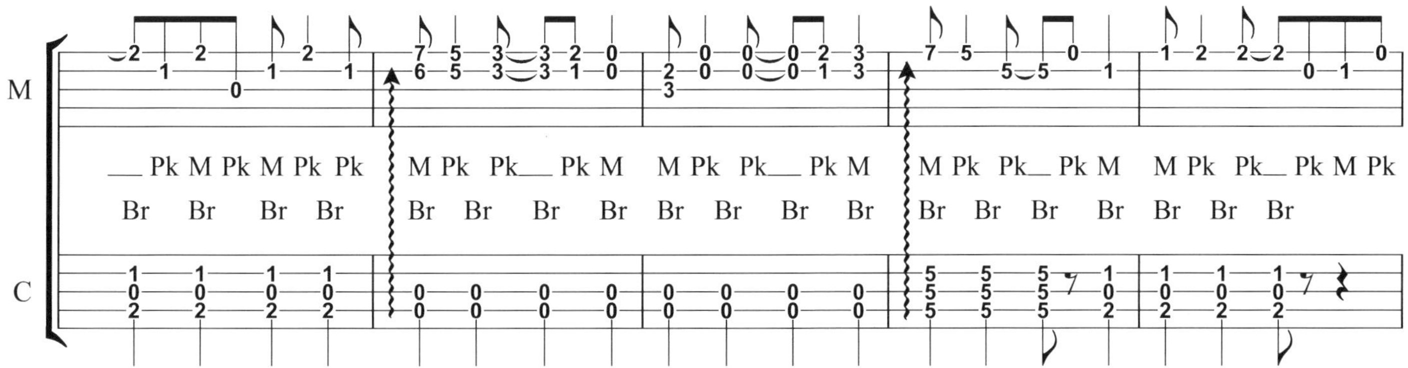
M
Pk M Pk M Pk Pk M Pk Pk Pk M M Pk Pk Pk M M Pk Pk Pk M M Pk Pk Pk M Pk
Br Br Br Br Br Br Br Br Br Br Br Br Br Br Br Br Br Br Br Br Br
C

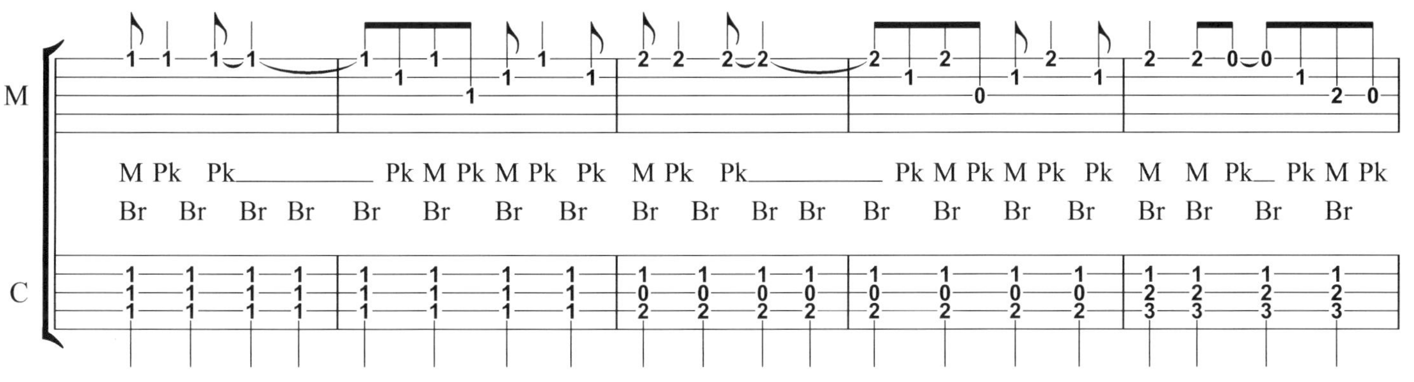
M
M Pk Pk Pk M Pk M Pk Pk M Pk Pk Pk M Pk M Pk Pk M M Pk Pk M Pk
Br Br Br Br Br Br Br Br Br Br Br Br Br Br Br Br Br Br Br Br
C

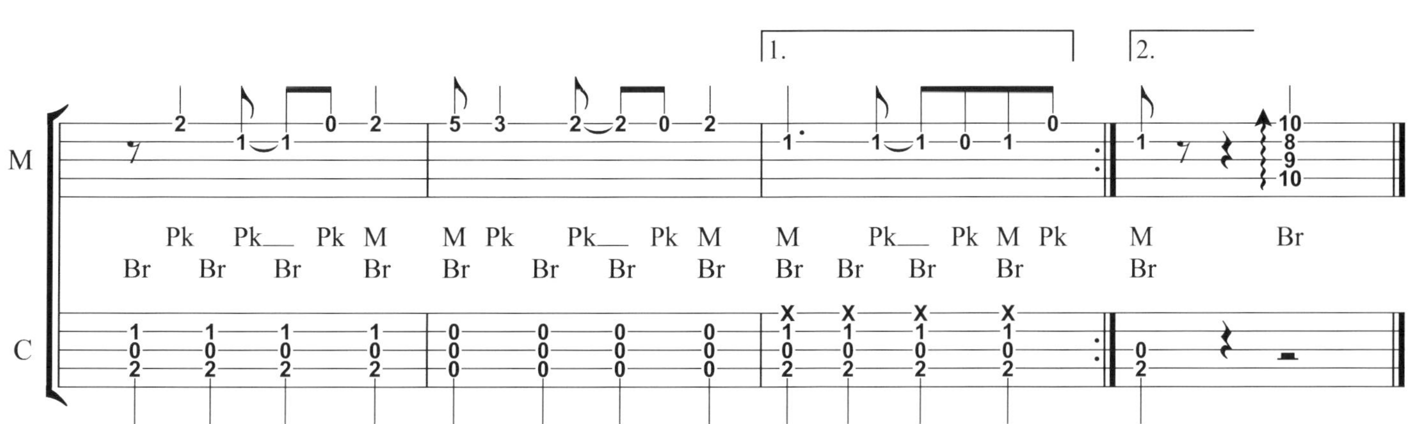
1.
2.
M
Pk Pk Pk M M Pk Pk Pk M M Pk Pk M Pk M Br
Br Br Br Br Br Br Br Br Br Br Br Br Br
C

Ragtime Dance

Scott Joplin
(arr. Steve Kahn)

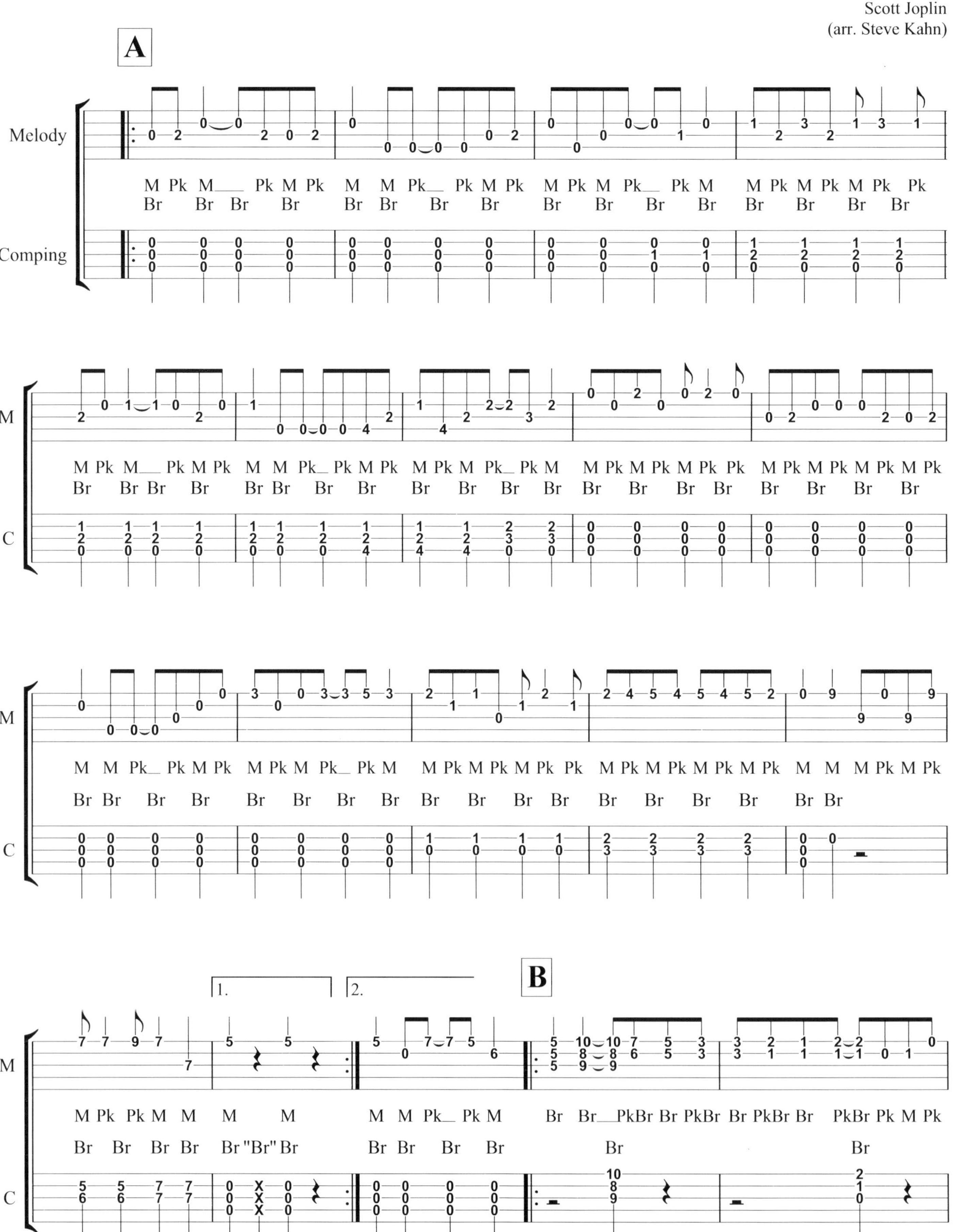

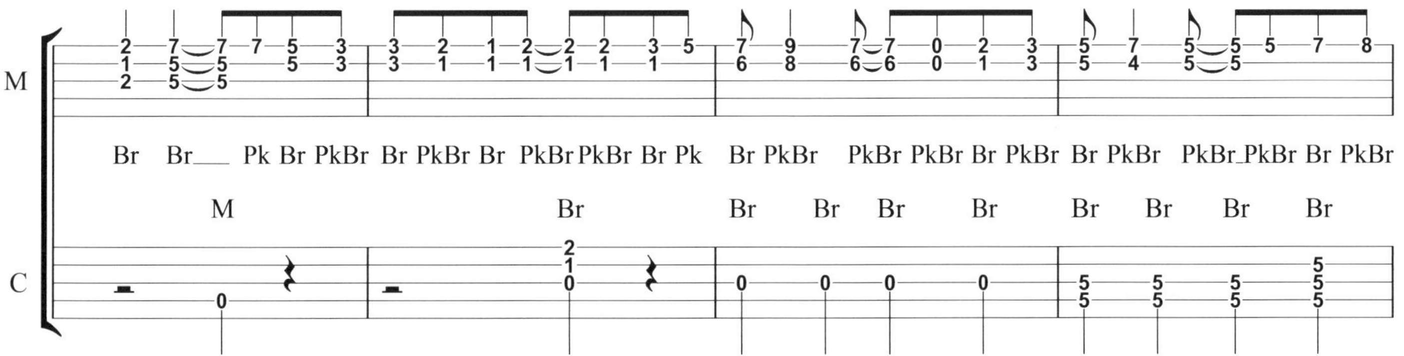

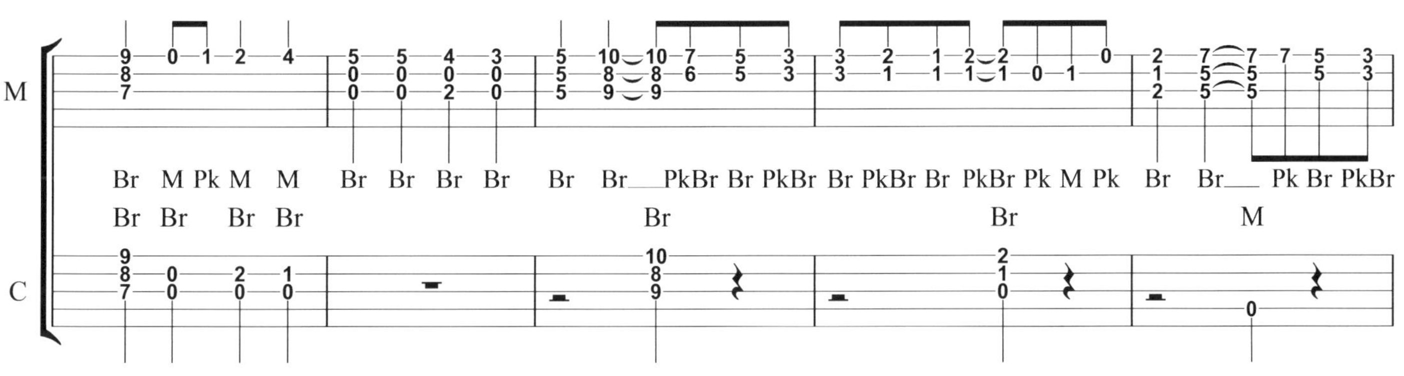

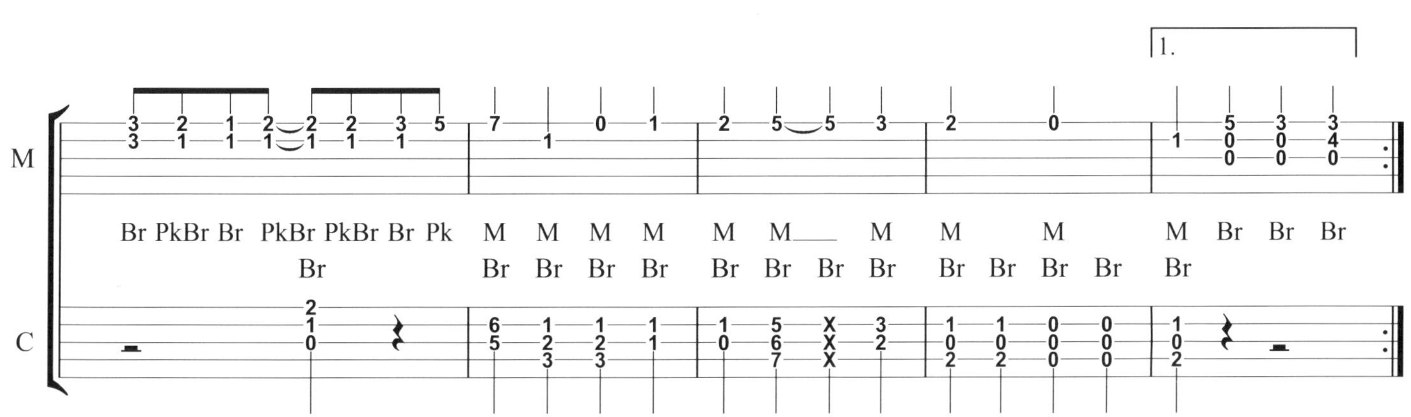

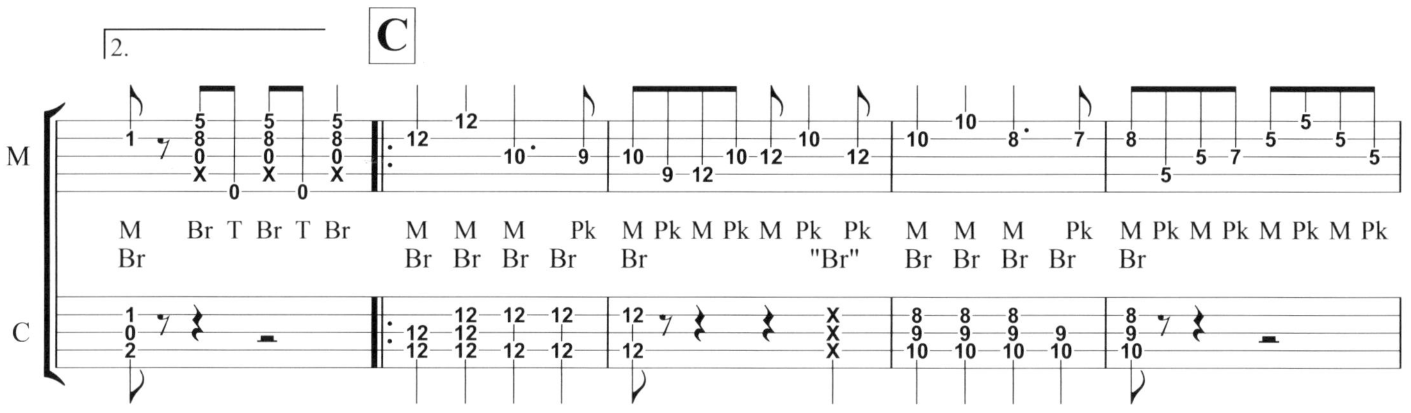
2.
C
M
C

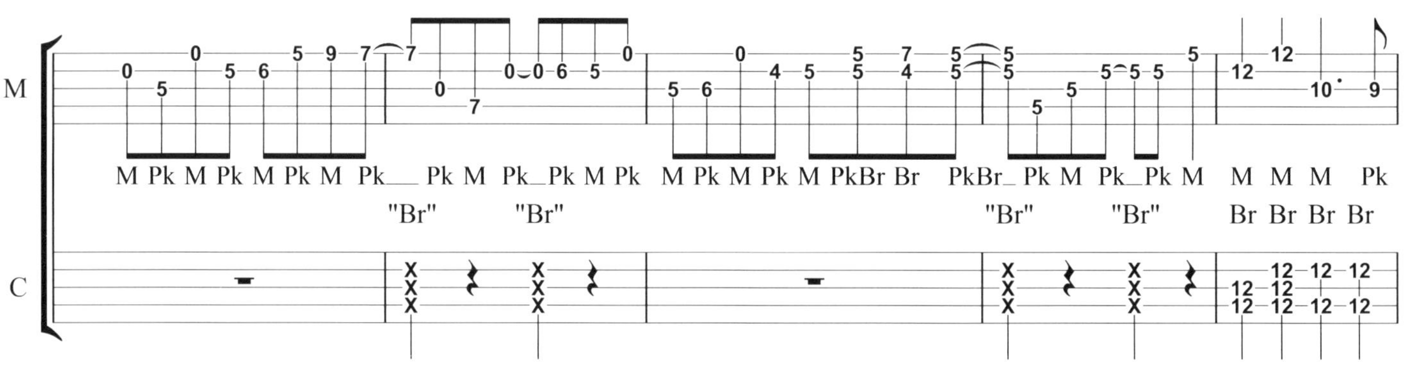
M
C

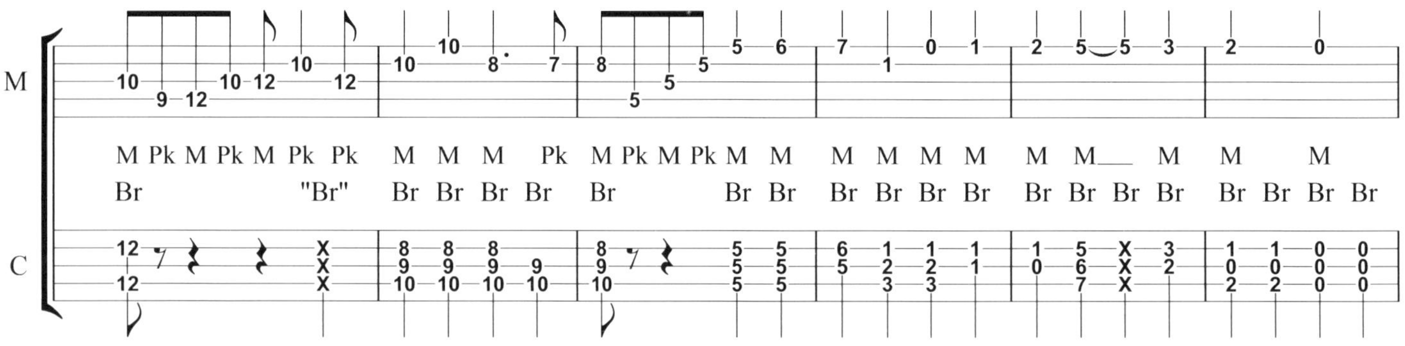
M
C

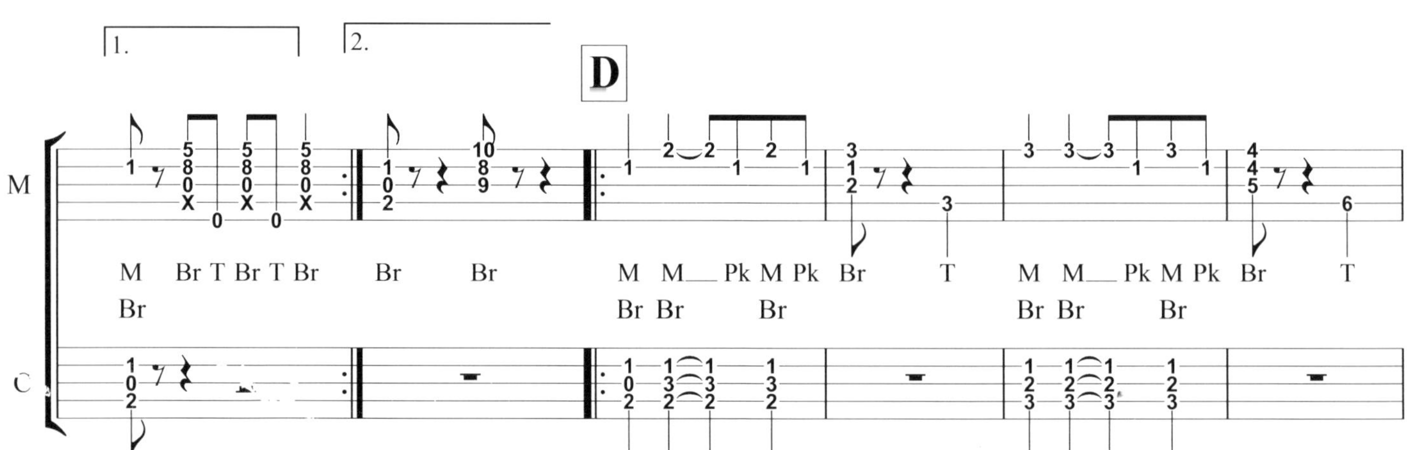
1.
2.
D
M
C

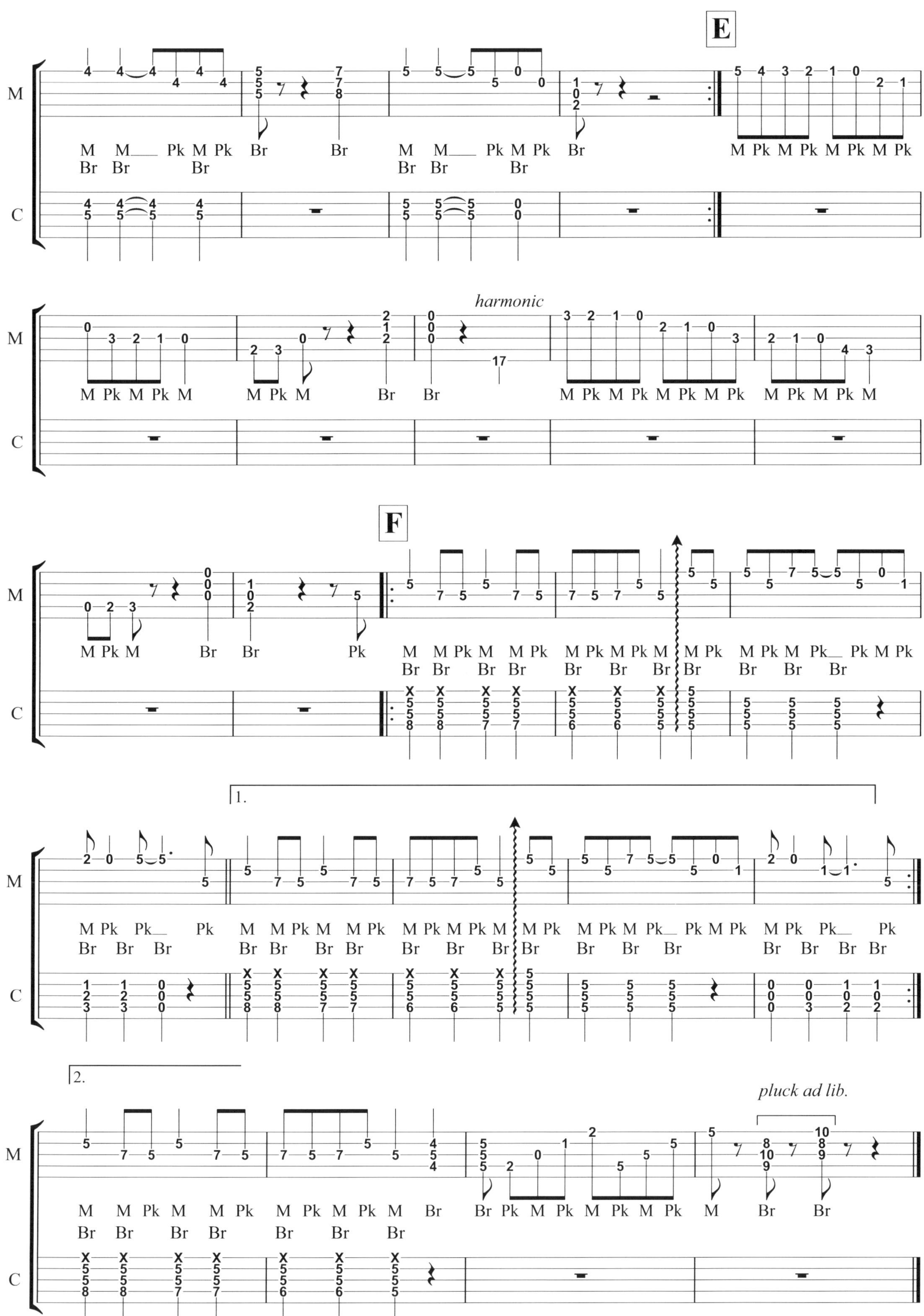
E
F
harmonic
1.
2.
pluck ad lib.
M
C

Solace

Scott Joplin
(arr. Steve Kahn)

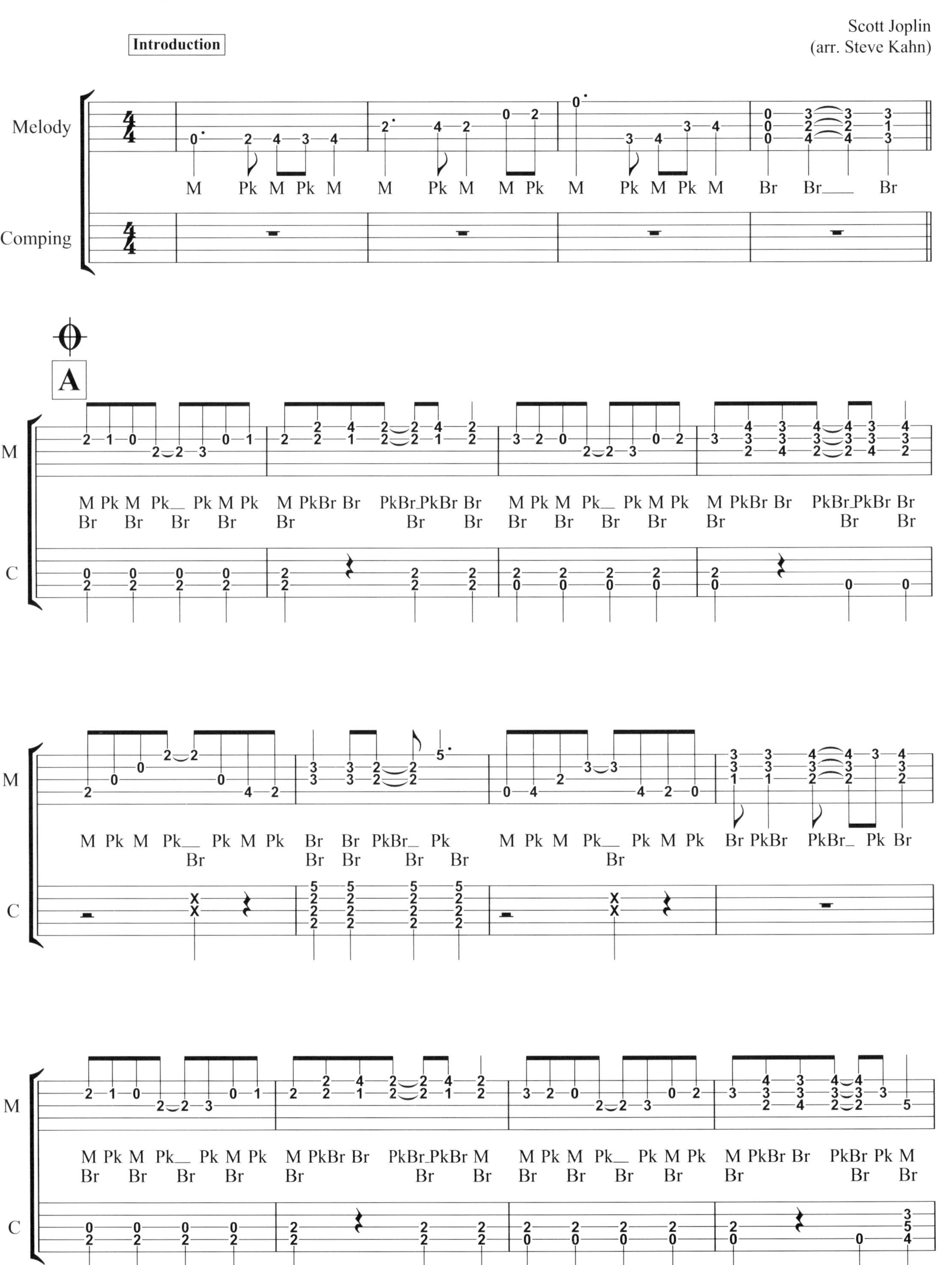

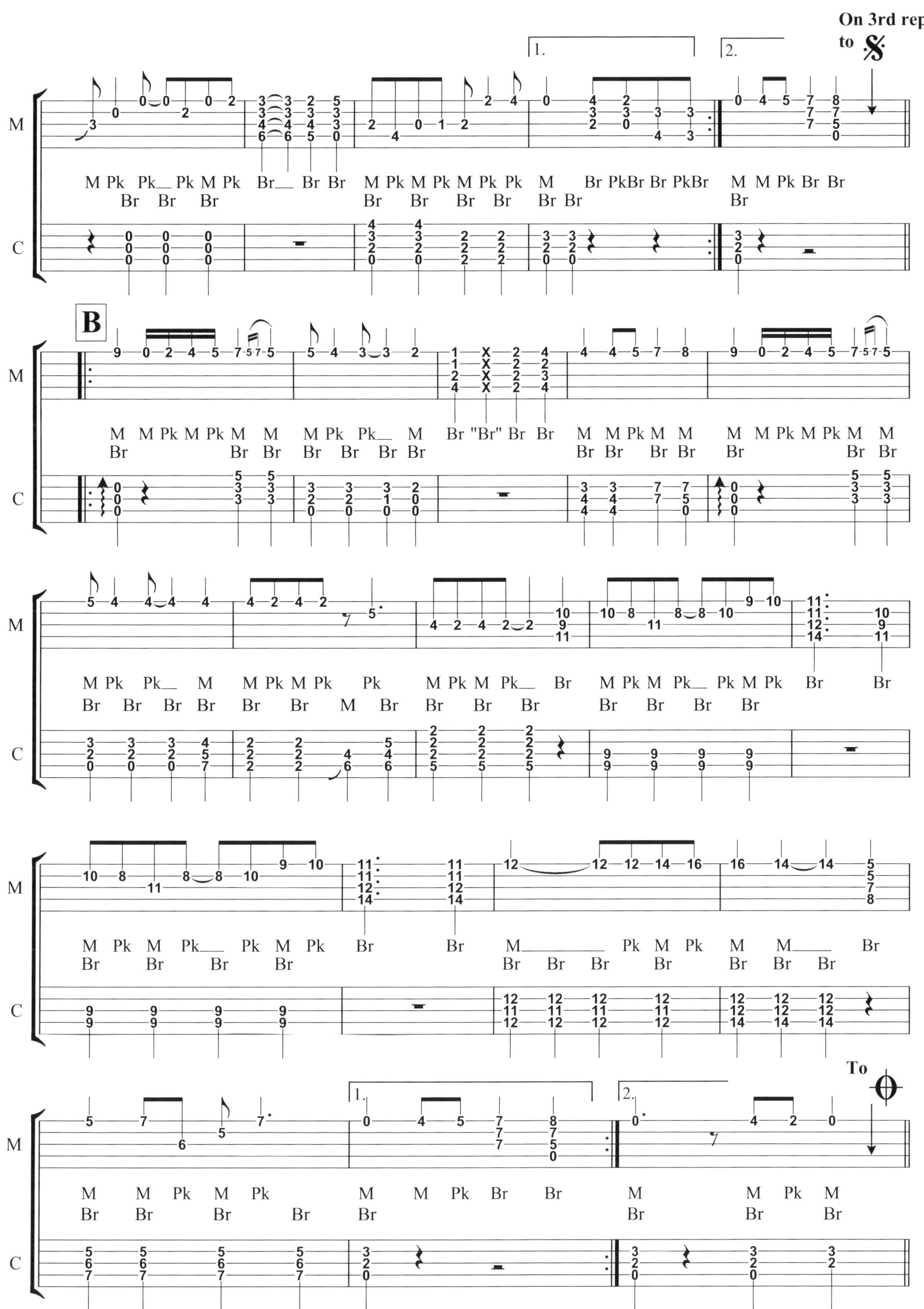
On 3rd repeat, to 𝄋
B
To 𝄌
M
C

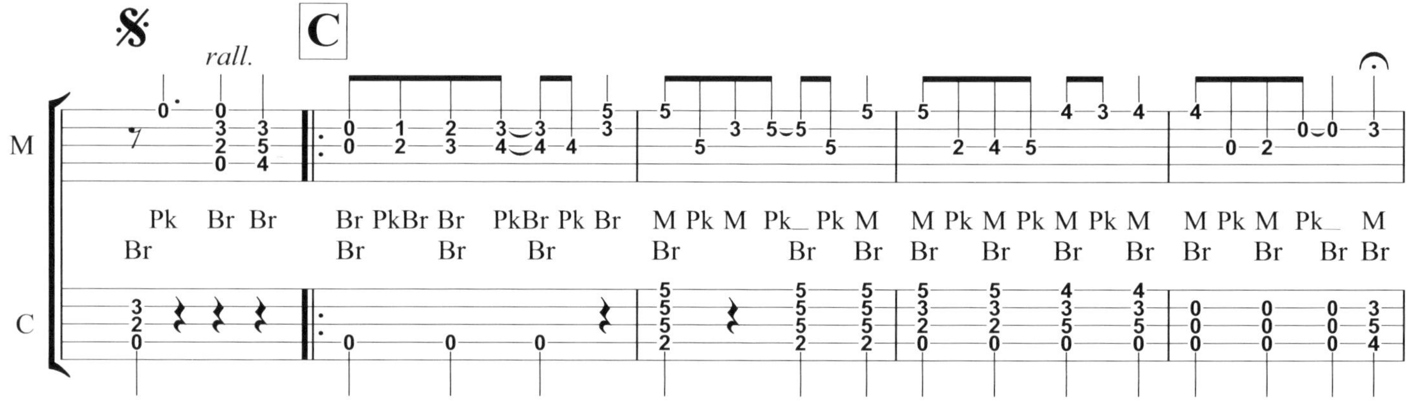
rall.
C
M
Pk Br Br Br PkBr Br PkBr Pk Br M Pk M Pk Pk M M Pk M Pk M Pk M M Pk M Pk M
Br Br Br Br Br Br Br Br Br Br Br Br Br Br Br
C

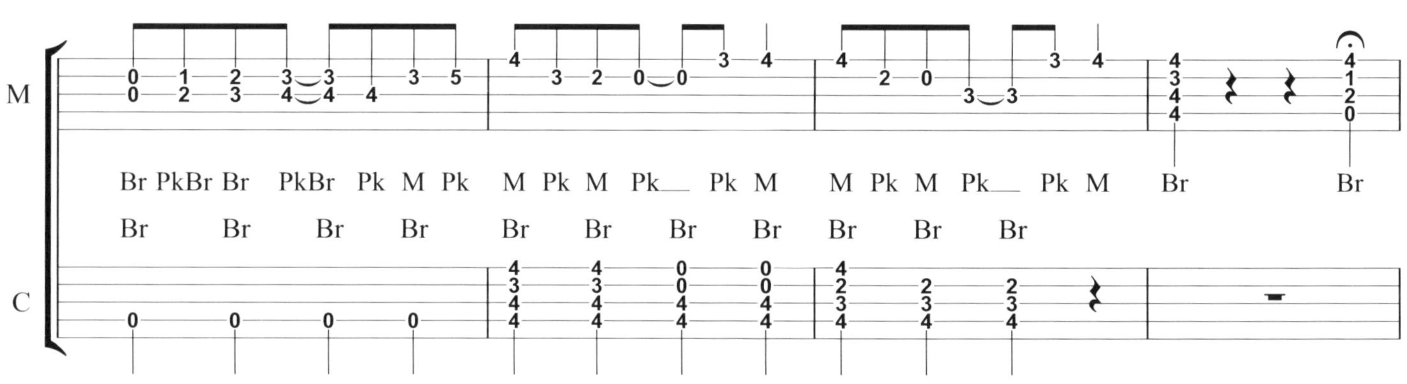
M
Br PkBr Br PkBr Pk M Pk M Pk M Pk Pk M M Pk M Pk Pk M Br Br
Br Br Br Br Br Br Br Br Br Br Br
C

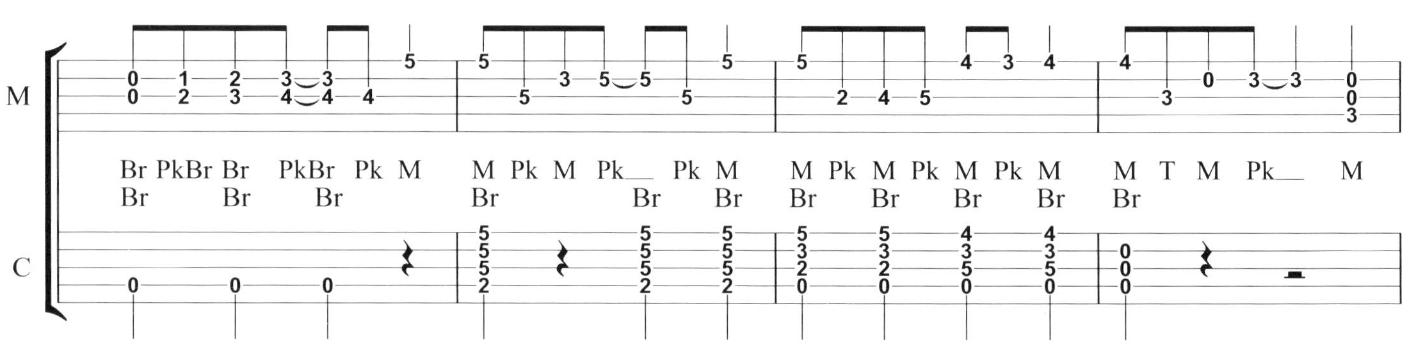
M
Br PkBr Br PkBr Pk M M Pk M Pk Pk M M Pk M Pk M Pk M M T M Pk M
Br Br Br Br Br Br Br Br Br Br Br
C

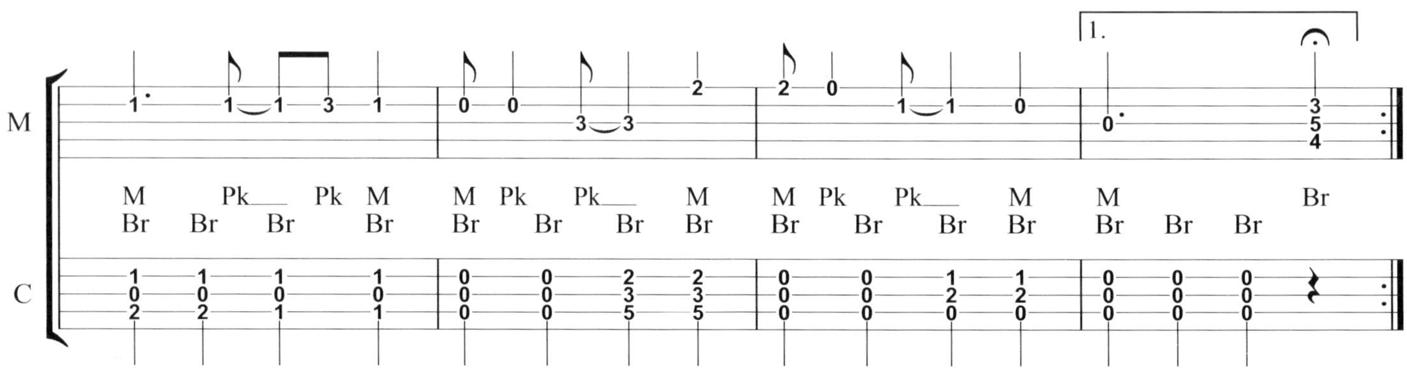
1.
M
M Pk Pk M M Pk Pk M M Pk Pk M M Br
Br Br Br Br Br Br Br Br Br Br Br Br Br Br Br
C

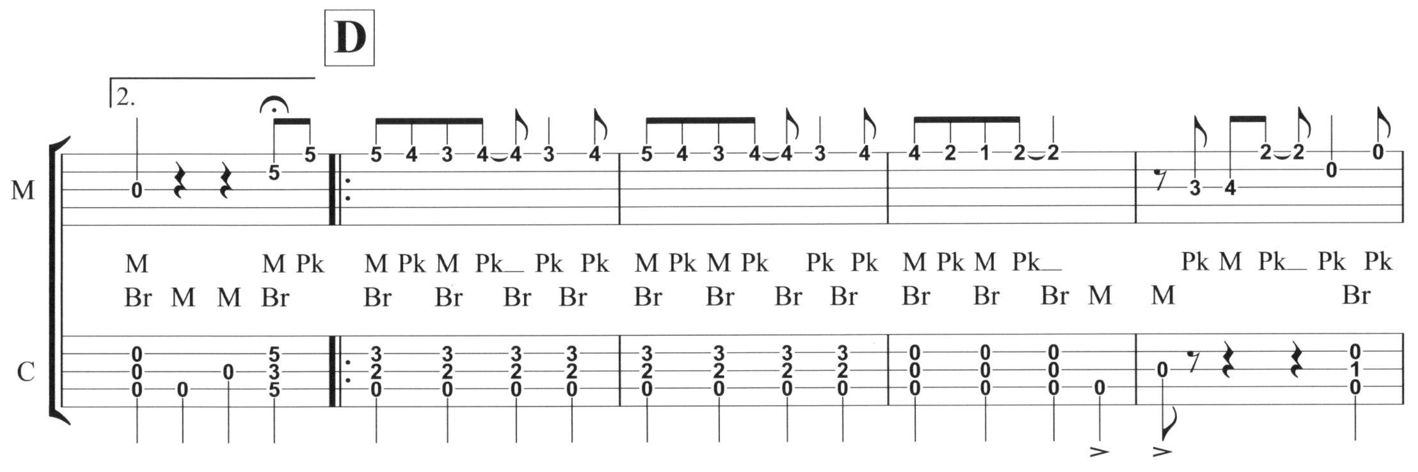
D
2.
M
C

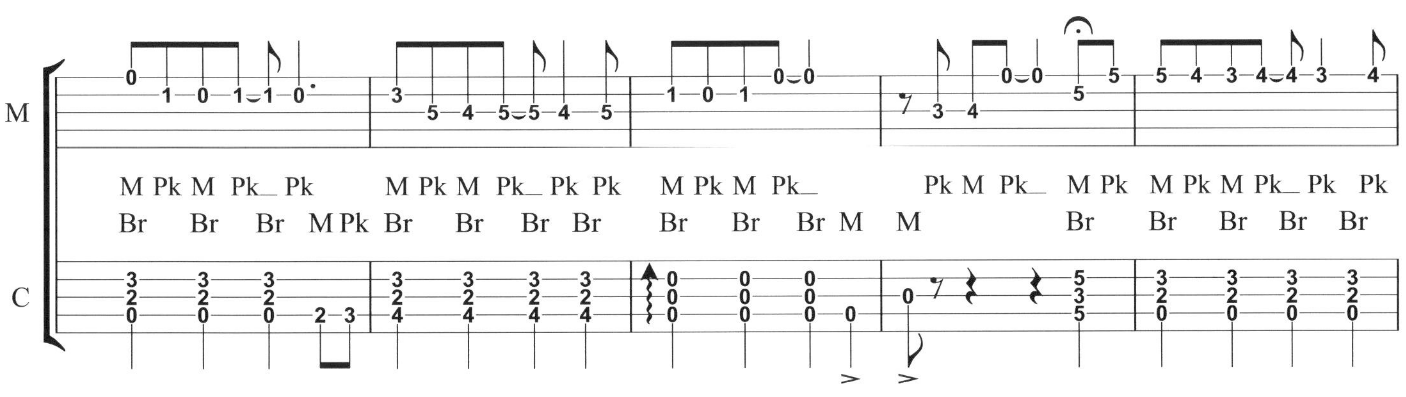
M
C

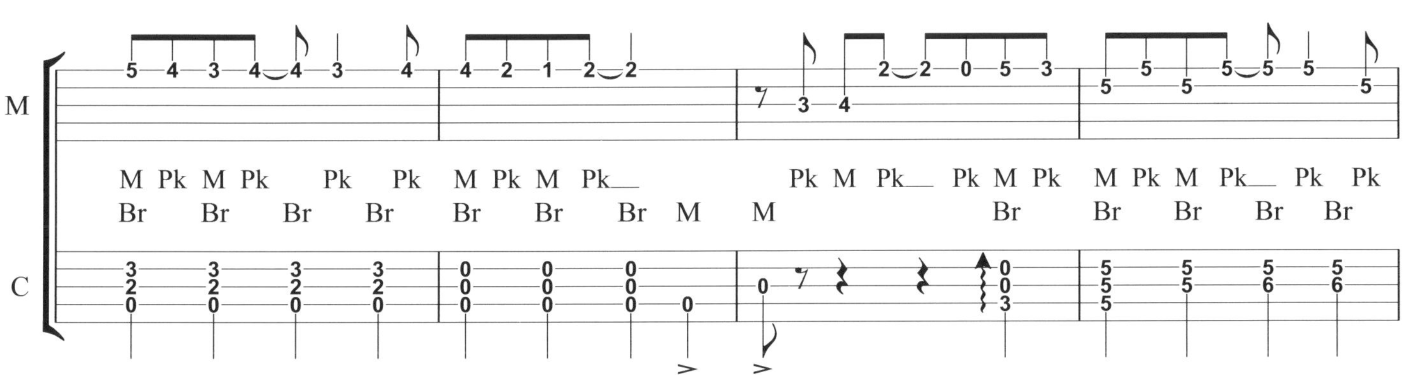
M
C

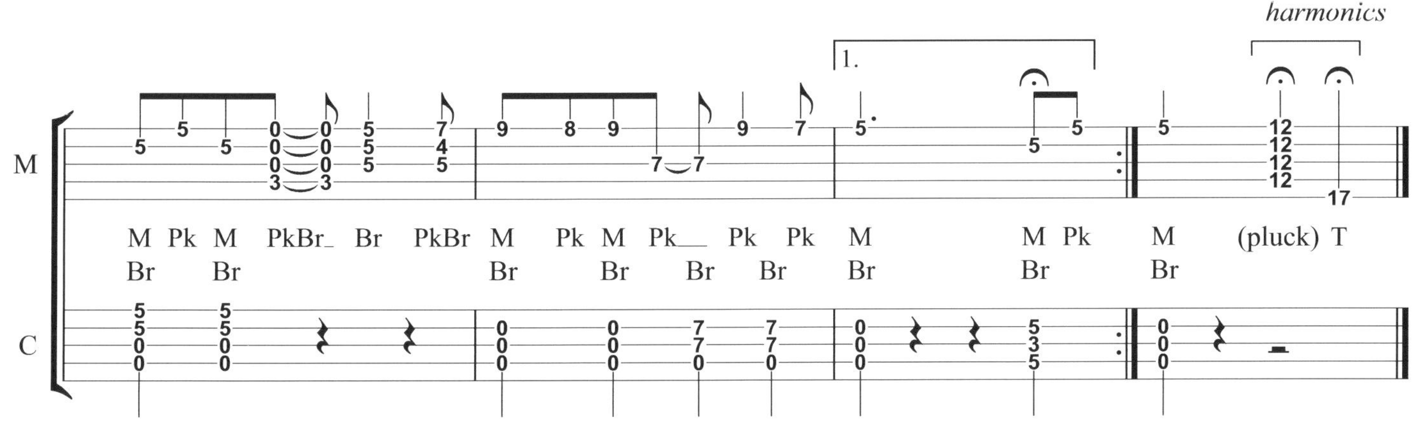
harmonics
1.
M
(pluck) T
C

Ragtime Fragment

(rest fretting hand thumb on 4th string ad lib.)

Steve Kahn

Melody

M Pk M Pk M Pk M Pk M Pk M Pk_ Pk M Pk M Pk M Pk M Pk M Pk M Pk_ Pk
Br Br Br Br Br Br Br Br Br Br Br Br Br Br Br Br

Comping

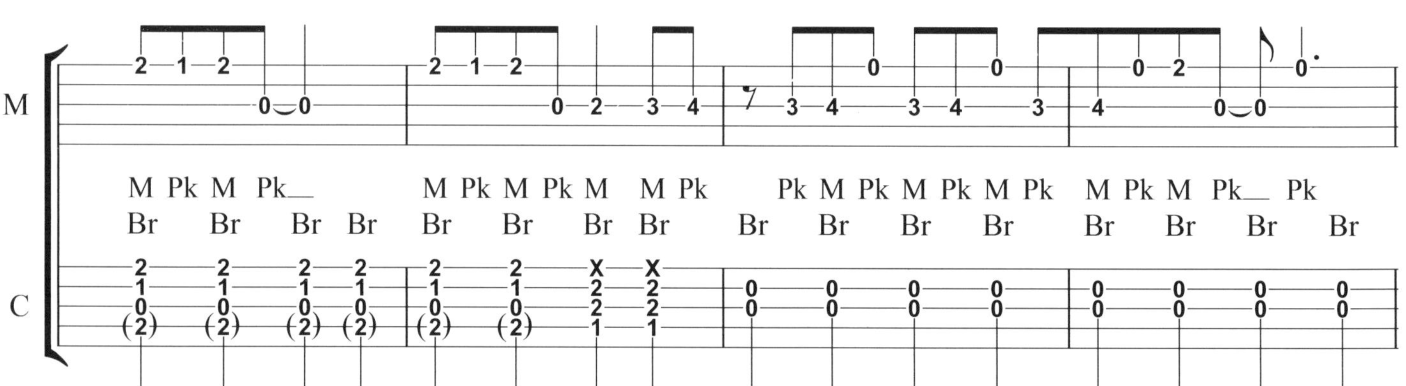

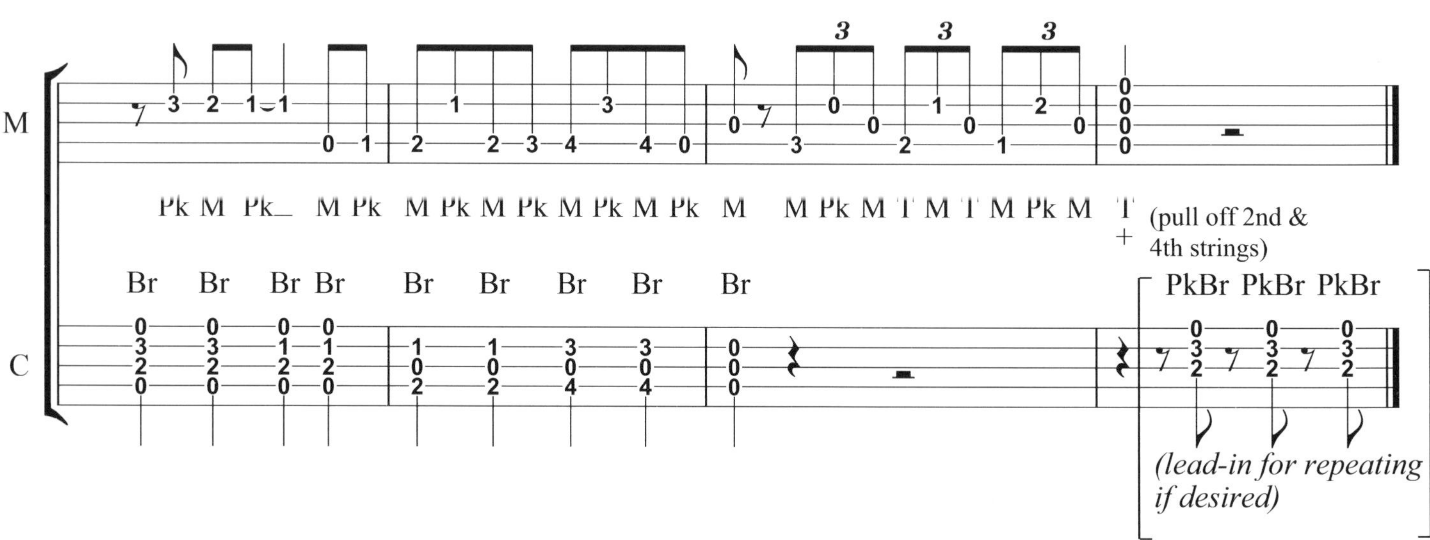

Steve Kahn's musical activities may be followed at *pawhammerbanjo.com* (5-string things) and *stevekmusic.net* (classical singing and composing). Thanks for checking out this book! I hope you've enjoyed it.